READY
RESOURCE

for

RELIEF
SOCIETY

READY
RESOURCE
for
RELIEF
SOCIETY

GOSPEL PRINCIPLES

PART ONE

compiled by

TRINA BOICE

CFI
Springville, Utah

This is not an official publication of The Church of Jesus Christ of Latter-day Saints. The opinions and views expressed herein belong solely to the author and do not necessarily represent the opinions or views of Cedar Fort, Inc. Permission for the use of sources, graphics, and photos is also solely the responsibility of the author.

ISBN 13: 978-1-59955-376-4

Published by CFI, an imprint of Cedar Fort, Inc., 2373 W. 700 S., Springville, UT, 84663
Distributed by Cedar Fort, Inc., www.cedarfort.com

Cover and book design by Jen Boss
Cover design © 2009 by Lyle Mortimer
Edited by Melissa J. Caldwell

Printed in the United States of America

10 9 8 7 6 5 4 3 2 1

Printed on acid-free paper

DEDICATION

For all of the wonderful Relief Society sisters I've had the privilege of serving with over the years who have taught me how to be a better wife, mother, sister, friend, daughter, and student of the gospel. Thank you to the Relief Society for always being there for me along my life's journey.

CONTENTS

ACKNOWLEDGMENTS

Thank you to Cedar Fort, Inc. for inviting me to share this book adventure with them! Thank you to all the faithful members of the Church who valiantly magnify their callings and give of their time and talents to bless those around them. Thank you to my husband and sons for all of their patient support and for washing all of those dishes while I'm busy writing books!

INTRODUCTION

The Ready Resource for Relief Society for 2010 is designed to be a helpful, inspiring resource to make lesson preparation easier and more exciting. Each chapter includes hymns appropriate for the lesson, quick summaries of the lesson material, quotes to supplement your class discussions, suggested artwork, and object lessons to add pizzazz to your lessons. In addition, each chapter contains a space for notes and a handout. Each handout is the same size as half a sheet of paper, so copying is quick and easy.

The Gospel Art Picture Kit is wonderful and can be purchased through Church distribution inexpensively. It makes a terrific addition to your family home evening lessons too! The kit includes 160 pictures that depict scripture stories or Church history events and illustrate gospel principles in action. The text on the back of each picture tells the story, offers scripture references, and provides additional information. The picture numbers in this book refer to the Gospel Art Picture Kit and not necessarily to the numbers your ward library may use.

Music can effectively teach and invite the Spirit almost better than any other teaching technique. Included with each lesson are suggestions for songs the class could sing or simply learn from by reading the lyrics.

Object lessons capture the class members' interest and increase their understanding by teaching the concept in a different way. The Savior often used physical objects that were familiar to His listeners to illustrate simple concepts. Each chapter offers an object lesson that could be an effective introduction to the topic or a fun way to keep the class engaged during class time.

The more you study and teach the gospel, the greater your own understanding will be. Use the scriptures each time you teach and encourage your class to sup from their pages. As you come to love the scriptures, your class will feel that passion and be inspired to feast upon them as well. Your task as a teacher is to invite the class to "come unto Christ." In order to do that effectively, you must create an atmosphere where the Holy Ghost will be welcome and able to testify to the hearts of your students. May you feel the Savior's love as you feed His sheep.

LESSON ONE

OUR HEAVENLY FATHER

Hymns

"Father in Heaven" — Hymns #133
"Father in Heaven, We Do Believe" — Hymns #180
"God of Our Fathers, We Come unto Thee" — Hymns #76
"I Know My Father Lives" — Children's Songbook #5
"I Need My Heavenly Father" — Children's Songbook #18
"My Heavenly Father Loves Me" — Children's Songbook #228

SUMMARY:

There *is* a God! He is a loving Heavenly Father who formed this Earth as a school for our learning and progression. He created everything in the universe and knows all things. He has a glorified body of flesh and bones, and we are made in His image. We are not only His greatest creation, we are His sons and daughters. By keeping His commandments, we can become like Him.

QUOTES:

ਡ "There is a great difference in believing or knowing that there is a God and in knowing God" (Bernard P. Brockbank, "Knowing God," *Ensign*, July 1972, 121–23).

ਡ "We *are* the children of God. That doctrine is not hidden away in an obscure verse. It is taught over and over again in scripture"

(Boyd K. Packer, "The Pattern of Our Parentage," *Ensign*, Nov. 1984, 6).

ᐒ "Belief in the fact that God exists is of first importance, but it is not *all* that is necessary in order to exercise an intelligent faith that will lead us back into his presence for eternal life with him" (N. Eldon Tanner, "A Basis for Faith in the Living God," *Ensign*, Nov. 1978, 46–49).

GOSPEL ART:

The First Vision – 403

OBJECT LESSONS:

ᐒ Begin by showing a padlock and asking what it can be used for. Then ask, "What good is a lock without a key?" Discuss how our lives only find meaning in a relationship with our Creator. God has made the Earth and us for a purpose. Jesus Christ is the key. Life without God is like a padlock without a key.

ᐒ Show a clock and discuss all of its moving parts. Discuss how just as the clock had to have been made by someone, so too have we been created by a divine maker.

ᐒ Ask the class "How many of you would like to see God?" Pass around a mirror and discuss how each one of us is made in His image and how we are truly divine. We can see God's reflection in Jesus; to see God clearly we need to learn more about the Savior.

ENSIGN TALKS

Gordon B. Hinckley, "In These Three I Believe," July 2006

Bernard P. Brockbank, "Knowing God," July 1972, 121–23

Boyd K. Packer, "The Pattern of Our Parentage," Nov. 1984, 66–69

N. Eldon Tanner, "A Basis for Faith in the Living God," Nov. 1978, 46–49

NOTES:

"There is a great difference in believing or **knowing** that there is a God and in **knowing** God."

—Bernard P. Brockbank

TO KNOW GOD BETTER THIS WEEK I WILL:

STUDY THE ATTRIBUTES OF GOD AND TRY TO BE MORE LIKE HIM.
D&C 88:41-44

★

SPEND MORE TIME IN MEANINGFUL PRAYER WITH HIM
JAMES 1:5

★

OBEY ALL OF HIS COMMANDMENTS TO SHOW MY LOVE FOR HIM
JOHN 14:15

★

DEMONSTRATE MORE FAITH
MOSIAH 4:9

★

BE STILL AND LISTEN FOR HIS PROMPTINGS
PSALMS 46:10

★

STUDY THE WORDS OF HIS PROPHETS
AMOS 3:7

"There is a great difference in believing or **knowing** that there is a God and in **knowing** God."

—Bernard P. Brockbank

TO KNOW GOD BETTER THIS WEEK I WILL:

STUDY THE ATTRIBUTES OF GOD AND TRY TO BE MORE LIKE HIM.
D&C 88:41-44

★

SPEND MORE TIME IN MEANINGFUL PRAYER WITH HIM
JAMES 1:5

★

OBEY ALL OF HIS COMMANDMENTS TO SHOW MY LOVE FOR HIM
JOHN 14:15

★

DEMONSTRATE MORE FAITH
MOSIAH 4:9

★

BE STILL AND LISTEN FOR HIS PROMPTINGS
PSALMS 46:10

★

STUDY THE WORDS OF HIS PROPHETS
AMOS 3:7

LESSON TWO

OUR HEAVENLY FAMILY

Hymns

"I Lived in Heaven" — *Children's Songbook* #4
"O God, the Eternal Father" — *Hymns* #175
"O My Father" — *Hymns* #292
"Our Father, by Whose Name" — *Hymns* #296
"O Thou, Before the World Began" — *Hymns* #189

SUMMARY:

Each one of us is a son or daughter of our loving Heavenly Father, who gave us the opportunity to come to the Earth to learn and grow. We lived before we came here as spirits, and we will continue to live after our bodies die. God created a plan of happiness for us so that we can become like Him. A Grand Council in heaven taught us that we would have agency to choose good or evil in mortality and that a Savior would be provided to help us overcome both spiritual and physical death.

QUOTES:

❧ "The Lord has carefully provided a plan of life called the plan of salvation. It comprises all of the laws, ordinances, principles, and doctrines required to complete our mortal journey and progress to a state of exaltation enjoyed by our Father in Heaven" (Duane

B. Gerrard, "The Plan of Salvation: A Flight Plan for Life," *Ensign*, Nov. 1997).

❧ "Our Heavenly Father has prepared a plan for us to be happy. His plan includes the Creation, the Fall, and the Atonement, with all the laws, covenants, and ordinances that allow us to be exalted and live forever as a family with God" (Adhemar Damiani, "The Merciful Plan of the Great Creator," *Ensign*, Mar. 2004, 8).

GOSPEL ART:

Elijah Restores the Power to Seal Families for Eternity – 417
Young Couple Going to the Temple – 609
Family Togetherness – 616

OBJECT LESSONS:

❧ Here is a new twist on a familiar object lesson to improve understanding about the plan of happiness. Hang a string across the room with small signs, designating the following periods of eternity: Premortal World, Mortality, Spirit Prison, Spirit Paradise, Resurrection, Final Judgment, Telestial Kingdom, Terrestrial Kingdom, Celestial Kingdom, Outer Darkness. Make large paper dolls for the class to hang on the string indicating where that person would be now. Use such labels on the dolls as:

—Born under the covenant in Australia and lived a valiant life from 1936–2009

—Born in Egypt in 300 BC, good person

—Delinquent teenager, born in 1992, who is currently in jail

—Early Christian who lived during Christ's day

—Nazi who served Hitler and killed thousands of Jews

—Moroni

—Citizens of the City of Enoch

—Your next door neighbor

⦿ To give the class a "taste" of the differences between the degrees of glory offer them bites of chocolate and ask which they'd prefer for eternity:

—No chocolate = Outer darkness

—Unsweetened chocolate = Telestial Kingdom

—Bitter-sweet chocolate = Terrestrial Kingdom

—Milk chocolate = Celestial Kingdom

ENSIGN TALKS

L. Tom Perry, "The Plan of Salvation," Nov. 2006

Robert D. Hales, "The Eternal Family," Nov. 1996

First Presidency, "The Origin of Man," Feb. 2002

Marcus B. Nash, "The Great Plan of Happiness," Nov. 2006

Quentin L. Cook, "Our Father's Plan—Big Enough for All His Children," May 2009

Earl C. Tingey, "The Great Plan of Happiness," May 2006

NOTES:

"THE LORD HAS CAREFULLY PROVIDED A PLAN
OF LIFE CALLED THE PLAN OF SALVATION.
IT COMPRISES ALL OF THE LAWS, ORDINANCES, PRINCIPLES,
AND DOCTRINES REQUIRED TO COMPLETE OUR MORTAL
JOURNEY AND PROGRESS TO A STATE OF EXALTATION
ENJOYED BY OUR FATHER IN HEAVEN."

—ELDER DUANE B. GERRARD

"THE LORD HAS CAREFULLY PROVIDED A PLAN
OF LIFE CALLED THE PLAN OF SALVATION.
IT COMPRISES ALL OF THE LAWS, ORDINANCES, PRINCIPLES,
AND DOCTRINES REQUIRED TO COMPLETE OUR MORTAL
JOURNEY AND PROGRESS TO A STATE OF EXALTATION
ENJOYED BY OUR FATHER IN HEAVEN."

—ELDER DUANE B. GERRARD

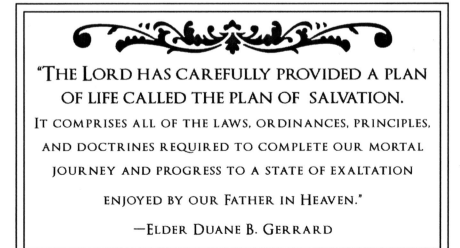

"THE LORD HAS CAREFULLY PROVIDED A PLAN
OF LIFE CALLED THE PLAN OF SALVATION.
IT COMPRISES ALL OF THE LAWS, ORDINANCES, PRINCIPLES,
AND DOCTRINES REQUIRED TO COMPLETE OUR MORTAL
JOURNEY AND PROGRESS TO A STATE OF EXALTATION
ENJOYED BY OUR FATHER IN HEAVEN."

—ELDER DUANE B. GERRARD

LESSON THREE

JESUS CHRIST, OUR CHOSEN LEADER AND SAVIOR

Hymns

"*Christ the Lord Is Risen Today*" — *Hymns #200*
"*God Loved Us So He Sent His Son*" — *Hymns #187*
"*I Believe in Christ* — *Hymns #134*
"*While of These Emblems We Partake*" — *Hymns #173 & #174*

SUMMARY:

Jesus Christ was chosen and foreordained to come to Earth to atone for our sins and to teach us how to return to our Heavenly Father. Because Satan was not selected, he rebelled and was cast out of God's presence, along with a third part of the hosts of heaven. These spirits were denied the right to receive mortal bodies and continue to wage war with the Savior's followers today. By following Jesus Christ, we can return to live with our eternal Father.

QUOTES:

❧ "Each of us has the responsibility to know the Lord, love Him, follow Him, serve Him, teach and testify of Him" (Russell M. Nelson, "Jesus the Christ: Our Master and More," *Ensign*, Apr. 2000, 4–17).

   ❥ "The soul that comes unto Christ dwells within a personal fortress, a veritable palace of perfect peace" (Jeffrey R. Holland, "Come unto Me," *Ensign*, Apr. 1998, 16–23).

   ❥ "The Redeemer loves you and will help you do the essential things that bring happiness now and forever" (Richard G. Scott, "Jesus Christ, Our Redeemer," *Ensign*, May 1997, 53–54, 59).

GOSPEL ART:

Isaiah Writes of Christ's Birth – 113
The Nativity – 201
Boy Jesus in the Temple – 205
Childhood of Jesus Christ – 206
John the Baptist Baptizing Jesus – 208
Calling of the Fishermen – 209
Christ Ordaining the Apostles – 211
Sermon on the Mount – 212
Christ Healing a Blind Man – 213
Stilling the Storm – 214
Jesus Blessing Jairus's Daughter – 215
Christ and the Children – 216
Mary and Martha – 219
Triumphal Entry – 223
Jesus Washing the Apostles' Feet – 226
Jesus Praying in Gethsemane – 227
The Betrayal of Jesus – 228
The Crucifixion – 230
Jesus' Tomb – 232
Mary and the Resurrected Lord – 233
Jesus Shows His Wounds – 234
Go Ye Therefore – 235
The Ascension of Jesus – 236
Jesus at the Door – 237

OBJECT LESSONS:

❧ Show the class some different kinds of keys: old-fashioned ones, key rings, hotel card keys, and so forth. Explain how the keys let you into appealing locations like fancy hotel rooms, luxury vehicles, and bank safes. Some people judge their lives by the keys they possess. For example, an education is the key to a good career. A car is a key to freedom. A good job is the key to power and wealth. A key to a large home represents success and security. There is only one key that opens the most important destination of all: Jesus Christ is the key to eternal life with Father in Heaven!

❧ Show objects that the class has to relate to Jesus Christ
    —Porch light: serves as a beacon to help us find our way home
    —Campfire: provides warmth and comfort
    —Lighthouse: Offers light in the darkness, offers perspective in the storm
    —Night light: banishes darkness and eliminates fear
    —Car headlights: lets us know where we are heading
    —Lights in a movie theater: a guide that can be followed
    —Light bulb: inspires us and brings us new light and understanding

ENSIGN TALKS:

Ezra Taft Benson, "Five Marks of the Divinity of Jesus Christ," Dec. 2001

Ezra Taft Benson, "Jesus Christ: Our Savior and Redeemer," June 1990

Russell M. Nelson, "Jesus the Christ: Our Master and More," Apr. 2000

Orson F. Whitney, "The Divinity of Jesus Christ," Dec. 2003

NOTES:

"EACH OF US HAS THE *responsibility* TO KNOW THE LORD, LOVE HIM, FOLLOW HIM, SERVE HIM, TEACH AND TESTIFY OF HIM."
—RUSSELL M. NELSON

"EACH OF US HAS THE *responsibility* TO KNOW THE LORD, LOVE HIM, FOLLOW HIM, SERVE HIM, TEACH AND TESTIFY OF HIM."
—RUSSELL M. NELSON

"EACH OF US HAS THE *responsibility* TO KNOW THE LORD, LOVE HIM, FOLLOW HIM, SERVE HIM, TEACH AND TESTIFY OF HIM."
—RUSSELL M. NELSON

LESSON FOUR

FREEDOM TO CHOOSE

"Choose the Right" — *Hymns #239*
"Choose the Right Way" — *Children's Songbook #160*
"Know This, That Every Soul Is Free" — *Hymns #240*

SUMMARY:

The right to choose between good and evil and to act for ourselves is called agency. By following Jesus Christ we are choosing eternal life and liberty. If we follow Satan we are selecting evil and eternal captivity. One of the purposes of mortality is to show which choices we'll make, so there must be opposition in all things in order for us to exercise agency. While we are free to make choices, we are not free to choose the consequences of our actions. What good is having someone who can walk on water if you don't follow in His footsteps?

QUOTES:

- "We are given the knowledge, the help, the enticement, and the freedom to choose the path of eternal safety and salvation. The choice to do so is ours" (Howard W. Hunter, "The Golden Thread of Choice," *Ensign*, Nov. 1989, 17–18).

ॐ "Ever and always [the Atonement] offers amnesty from transgression and from death if we will but repent. . . . Repentance is the key with which we can unlock the prison from inside . . . , and agency is ours to use it" (Boyd K. Packer, "Atonement, Agency, Accountability," *Ensign*, May 1988, 69–72).

GOSPEL ART:

Mary and Martha – 219
The Prodigal Son – 220

OBJECT LESSONS:

ॐ Set up a game of "Jenga" or "Stak Attack," or place wooden blocks in a weave pattern so you can pull out the blocks and re-stack them on top. Invite class members to remove one of the blocks and mention a commandment we need to obey. As you play the game, discuss the consequences of disobedience. Eventually, the tower will fall. Compare this to our spirituality when we continue to choose evil over good.

ॐ Give a volunteer a bag marked "Good Choices" (filled with Legos). Give another volunteer a second bag marked "Bad Choices" (filled with broken sticks). Ask them to build the best house they can with what they were given. Talk about how it's difficult to build a good life built out of bad choices.

ॐ

ENSIGN TALKS:

Robert D. Hales, "To Act for Ourselves: The Gift and Blessings of Agency," May 2006

Wolfgang H. Paul, "The Gift of Agency," May 2006

Howard W. Hunter, "The Golden Thread of Choice," Nov. 1989

Delbert L. Stapley, "Using Our Free Agency," May 1975

Boyd K. Packer, "Atonement, Agency, Accountability," May 1988

Spencer J. Condie, "Agency: the Gift of Choices," Sept. 1995

NOTES:

EVER AND ALWAYS THE *atonement* OFFERS AMNESTY FROM TRANSGRESSION AND FROM DEATH IF WE WILL BUT REPENT... REPENTANCE IS THE *key* WITH WHICH WE CAN UNLOCK THE PRISON FROM INSIDE ... AND *agency* IS OURS TO USE IT.

—BOYD K. PACKER

EVER AND ALWAYS THE *atonement* OFFERS AMNESTY FROM TRANSGRESSION AND FROM DEATH IF WE WILL BUT REPENT... REPENTANCE IS THE *key* WITH WHICH WE CAN UNLOCK THE PRISON FROM INSIDE ... AND *agency* IS OURS TO USE IT.

—BOYD K. PACKER

LESSON FIVE

THE CREATION

"All Things Bright and Beautiful" — Children's Songbook #231
"If You Could Hie to Kolob" — Hymns #284
"Praise to the Lord, the Almighty" — Hymns #72
"Praise the Lord with Heart and Voice" — Hymns #73

SUMMARY:

Our spirits lived with Heavenly Father and were given a physical body when we came here on Earth so that we could become like Him. Under the direction of the Father, Jesus Christ created this world for us to have joy, be tested, create families, and prove ourselves worthy to inherit eternal life. Not only are we God's greatest creation, but we are also His family!

QUOTES:

❧ "The purposes of the Creation, the Fall, and the Atonement all converge on the sacred work done in temples of The Church of Jesus Christ of Latter-day Saints" (Russell M. Nelson, "The Atonement," *Ensign*, Nov. 1996, 33–36).

❧ "The very Creation of the earth is a manifestation of God's love for us" (Mark J. Nielsen, "The Wonder of the Creation," *Ensign*, Mar. 2004, 60–65).

❧ "Grand as it is, planet Earth is part of something even grander— that great plan of God. Simply summarized, the earth was created that families might be" (Russell M. Nelson, "The Creation," *Ensign*, May 2000, 84–86).

GOSPEL ART KIT:

Creation — Living Creatures – 100
The World – 600

OBJECT LESSONS:

❧ Hold up a 500-piece puzzle with a beautiful scene on it. Tell the class you are going to create that scene for them in the room. Explain that you can't create it out of nothing, but you will use the matter provided (puzzle pieces). Yell "Bang!" and toss all 500 pieces all over the classroom. Look confused and ask the class why it didn't work. Explain that someone needs to organize the matter. Our beautiful world wasn't created by accident, but by a loving Heavenly Father.

❧ Tell the class that for the last few decades millions of dollars have been poured into aviation research. In Europe, millions were spent developing the Concord—a commercial aircraft that could fly faster than sound. In the USA, a huge team of scientists and engineers developed the space shuttle. Another team developed the stealth bomber that is specially designed to be invisible to radar systems. Then tell them about a flying machine that incorporates far superior, amazing technology than all the governments, money, and military have been able to come up with. This machine can take off and land sideways on a vertical surface. It can take off with such astounding acceleration and has such a sophisticated early warning system that if it senses an enemy attack while on the ground, it can take off and be out of range within in a fraction of a second. Tell them that you have a picture of one these fabulous flying machines. Ask if the class would you like to see it and then show them a picture of a common housefly. This world, with all of its miraculous creations, was designed by God, not by chance.

ENSIGN TALKS:

Russell M. Nelson, "The Creation," May 2000

M. Russell Ballard, "The Handiwork of God," Mar. 2006

Mark J. Nielsen, "The Wonder of the Creation," Mar. 2004

Keith Meservy, "Four Accounts of the Creation," Jan. 1986

Robert J. Woodford, "In the Beginning: A Latter-day Perspective," Jan. 1998

Bruce R. McConkie, "Christ and the Creation," June 1982

NOTES:

"GRAND AS IT IS, PLANET EARTH
IS PART OF SOMETHING
EVEN GRANDER—
that great plan of God.
SIMPLY SUMMARIZED, THE
EARTH WAS CREATED
that families might be."

—RUSSELL M. NELSON

"GRAND AS IT IS, PLANET EARTH
IS PART OF SOMETHING
EVEN GRANDER—
that great plan of God.
SIMPLY SUMMARIZED, THE
EARTH WAS CREATED
that families might be."

—RUSSELL M. NELSON

LESSON SIX

THE FALL OF
ADAM AND EVE

"A Mighty Fortress Is Our God" — *Hymns #68*

SUMMARY:

Adam and Eve were chosen to come to Earth first and to bring mortality into the world. They were given physical life (mortal bodies) and spiritual life (they lived in the presence of God), but after partaking of the fruit of the tree of knowledge of good and evil, their condition changed. Physical death and a separation from Heavenly Father resulted from their transgression, requiring a Savior to redeem us all. Their Fall was a necessary part of God's great plan of happiness. Because of them, we have the opportunity to experience mortality and learn the lessons of life.

QUOTES:

❧ "The Fall was not a disaster. It wasn't a mistake or an accident. It was a deliberate part of the plan of salvation" (Bruce C. Hafen,

"The Atonement: All for All," *Ensign*, May 2004, 97–99).

  "The Fall was a 'glorious necessity to open the doorway toward eternal life' " (Jess L. Christensen, "The Choice That Began Mortality," *Ensign*, Jan. 2002, 36–38; or *Liahona*, Aug. 2002, 38–41).

GOSPEL ART:

Adam and Eve – 101
Adam and Eve Teaching Their Children – 119

OBJECT LESSONS:

  Show the class a $100 bill and ask who would like it. Then wrinkle the bill up and ask them again. Of course, they'll still say they want it. Now throw it on the floor and rub it with your shoe. When they still want it, ask them if they'd want it if you put it in the mud or the toilet. Tell them this is exactly how much Jesus Christ wants us! No matter what we've done, we're still worth the same to Him. Because of His love for us, the Savior created the world for us and was willing to be born to pay the price for sin. Explain that the Fall was a part of the plan and had to occur in order for us to pass through mortality on the way to eternity.

  Give a volunteer a bowl of pudding and tell her she can eat as much pudding as she wants without bending her elbows. When she discovers she's unable, ask another volunteer to help her. There are some things we simply can't do on our own. Adam and Eve had to be born first before we would be able to come to Earth. Because we would all sin in mortality we would need the Savior to atone for our sins.

ENSIGN TALKS:

Joseph Fielding Smith, "Adam's Role In Bringing Us Mortality," Jan. 2006

Spencer J. Condie, "The Fall and Infinite Atonement," Jan. 1996

Gerald N. Lund, "The Fall of Man and His Redemption," Jan. 1990

Donald K. Jarvis, "Leaving Eden: A Lesson For Parents," Feb. 1991

Russell M. Nelson, "Lessons From Eve," Nov. 1987

Robert J. Woodford, "In the Beginning: A Latter-day Perspective," Jan. 1998

NOTES:

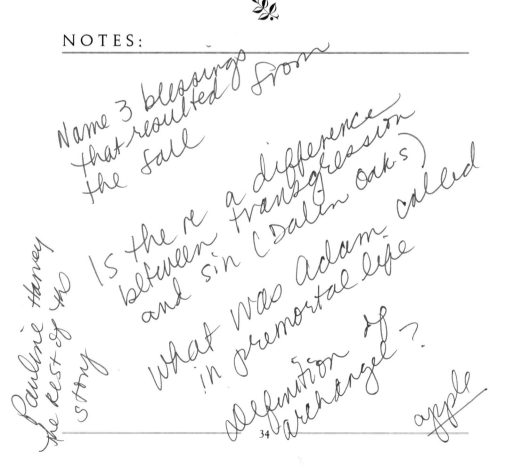

Name 3 blessings that resulted from the fall

Is there a difference between transgression and sin (Dalin Oaks)

What was Adam called in premortal life

definition of archangel?

Pauline Harvey The rest of the story

apple

"The Fall was a glorious necessity to open the doorway toward *eternal life.*"

—Jess Christensen

"The Fall was a glorious necessity to open the doorway toward *eternal life.*"

—Jess Christensen

"The Fall was a glorious necessity to open the doorway toward *eternal life.*"

—Jess Christensen

"The Fall was a glorious necessity to open the doorway toward *eternal life.*"

—Jess Christensen

2 plastic
2 real eggs

Will they ever die

LESSON SEVEN

THE HOLY GHOST

Hymns

"Lord, Accept into Thy Kingdom" — Hymns #236
"Testimony" — Hymns #137
"The Holy Ghost" — Children's Songbook #105
"The Spirit of God" — Hymns #2
"The Still Small Voice" — Children's Songbook #106

SUMMARY:

The Holy Ghost has been sent to us by a loving Heavenly Father to provide comfort, guidance, and a witness for truth. The Holy Ghost is a member of the Godhead and has a distinct mission to testify of the Father and the Son to our minds and hearts. The Holy Ghost is a personage of spirit that speaks to our souls and by its power we are able to understand and live the gospel of Jesus Christ.

QUOTES:

- "We need the help of the Holy Ghost if we are to make our way safely through what the Apostle Paul called the 'perilous times' in which we now live" (Gerald N. Lund, "Opening Our Hearts," *Ensign*, May 2008).

- "When the Prophet Joseph Smith was asked 'wherein [the LDS

Church] differed . . . from the other religions of the day,' he replied that it was in 'the gift of the Holy Ghost by the laying on of hands, . . . [and] that all other considerations were contained in the gift of the Holy Ghost' " (James E. Faust, "The Light in Their Eyes," *Ensign*, Nov. 2005).

- "The Holy Ghost . . . is our comforter, our direction finder, our communicator, our interpreter, our witness, and our purifier— our infallible guide and sanctifier" (Dallin H. Oaks, " 'Always Have His Spirit,' " *Ensign*, Nov. 1996, 59–61).

- "This powerful gift entitles the leaders and all worthy members of the Church to enjoy the gifts and companionship of the Holy Ghost, a member of the Godhead whose function is to inspire, reveal, and teach all things" (James E. Faust, "Communion with the Holy Spirit," *Ensign*, Mar. 2002, 2–7).

GOSPEL ART:

John the Baptist Baptizing Jesus – 208

OBJECT LESSONS:

- Have the class listen to the voices of apostles and prophets and let them guess whose voices they are. Talk about how it is much easier to recognize a voice when you are familiar with it. Play some voices of families in your ward. We need to spend time in the scriptures and in prayer in order to recognize the voice of the Lord through the Holy Ghost.

- Show the class a variety of objects that involve air in some way: balloons, a bicycle tire, hair dryer, inflatable balls, air pump, aerosol can, fan, soap bubbles, etc. Ask the class what they have in common. Explain that while we can't see air, we know it's there because of the effect it has on each of those objects. We can't see the Holy Ghost because it doesn't have a physical body, but we can feel its power and influence.

&» Put a pile of cushions on the floor with a dried pea hidden underneath. Get some volunteers to sit on the cushions and guess what is hidden underneath. You can even tell the class the story about the princess and the pea. The Holy Ghost makes us more sensitive to spiritual things. We are truly sons and daughters of a king.

ENSIGN TALKS:

Douglas L. Callister, "Seeking The Spirit of God." Nov. 2000
James E. Faust, "The Light in Their Eyes," Nov. 2005
Neal A. Maxwell, "The Holy Ghost: Glorifying Christ," July 2002
James E. Faust, "Communion With The Holy Spirit," Mar. 2002
Loren C. Dunn, "Fire and the Holy Ghost," June 1995

NOTES:

Are you in range of the Holy Ghost?

THE STRENGTH OF YOUR SPIRITUAL SIGNAL CAN BE DETERMINED BY:

- Prayer
- Scripture Study
- Christlike Service
- Church Attendance
- Obeying the Commandments
- Language (profanity/gossip)
- Music Choices
- Entertainment Choices
- Word of Wisdom
- Self-mastery

THIS WEEK I WILL WORK ON: _____

Are you in range of the Holy Ghost?

THE STRENGTH OF YOUR SPIRITUAL SIGNAL CAN BE DETERMINED BY:

- Prayer
- Scripture Study
- Christlike Service
- Church Attendance
- Obeying the Commandments
- Language (profanity/gossip)
- Music Choices
- Entertainment Choices
- Word of Wisdom
- Self-mastery

THIS WEEK I WILL WORK ON: _____

Are you in range of the Holy Ghost?

THE STRENGTH OF YOUR SPIRITUAL SIGNAL CAN BE DETERMINED BY:

- Prayer
- Scripture Study
- Christlike Service
- Church Attendance
- Obeying the Commandments
- Language (profanity/gossip)
- Music Choices
- Entertainment Choices
- Word of Wisdom
- Self-mastery

THIS WEEK I WILL WORK ON: _____

LESSON EIGHT

PRAYING TO OUR
HEAVENLY FATHER

Hymns

"*Before Thee, Lord, I Bow My Head*" — *Hymns #158*
"*Come unto Him*" — *Hymns #114*
"*Did You Think to Pray?*" — *Hymns #140*
"*Prayer Is the Soul's Sincerest Desire*" — *Hymns #145*
"*Sweet Hour of Prayer*" — *Hymns #142*

SUMMARY:

Prayer is the vehicle we can use to communicate with our Father in Heaven. We are commanded to pray always unto the Father and only Him. We can pray either vocally or silently, asking for guidance and strength, confessing our sins, showing gratitude, and requesting specific blessings. We should pray individually and as families each day. God answers our prayers by granting us increased ability or by inspiring others to help us. As we pray, we draw closer to our Heavenly Father until His will is the same as ours.

QUOTES:

>   "Our Father in Heaven has promised us peace in times of trial and has provided a way for us to come to Him in our need. He has given us the privilege and power of prayer" (Rex D. Pinegar,

"Peace through Prayer," *Ensign*, May 1993, 65–68).

æ "A return to the old pattern of prayer, family prayer in the homes of the people, is one of the basic medications that would check the dread disease that is eroding the character of our society" (Gordon B. Hinckley, "The Blessings of Family Prayer," *Ensign*, Feb. 1991, 2–5).

æ "Men and women of integrity, character, and purpose have ever recognized a power higher than themselves and have sought through prayer to be guided by such power" (Thomas S. Monson, "The Prayer of Faith," *Ensign*, Aug. 1995, 2–7).

æ "I can think of no greater teaching to our children than that of the power of prayer" (L. Tom Perry, " 'Our Father Which Art in Heaven,' " *Ensign*, Nov. 1983, 11–13).

GOSPEL ART:

Jesus Praying in Gethsemane – 227
Enos Praying – 305
Moroni Hides the Plates in the Hill Cumorah – 320
The First Vision – 403
Young Boy Praying – 605
Family Prayer – 606

OBJECT LESSONS:

æ Invite the class to share their experiences of trying to find a moment in their hectic lives for personal prayer. Before the discussion ask a volunteer in private to keep raising her hand while you ignore her. You could even acknowledge her but tell her you need to say a few more things before she can talk. Finally, when you call on her, have her tell the class of your plan and explain that sometimes our prayers are like that; we do all of the talking and don't let the Lord participate in the discussion!

⇒ As you walk into the room, talk loudly on your mobile phone as if you are talking to a friend. Talk about your plans for the day, the things you need to do, and then ask for advice. Ask the class to compare your conversation to prayer. Remind them that talking on a cell phone is different from prayer in the following ways:
— God is never out of range.
— We never "lose the signal."
— The battery never runs dead.
— We never run out of minutes.
— We don't have to remember God's number . . . just talk!

ENSIGN TALKS:

David A. Bednar, "Pray Alway," Nov. 2008
Dallin H. Oaks, "The Language of Prayer," May 1993
Russell M. Nelson, "Lessons from the Lord's Prayers," May 2009
James E. Faust, "The Lifeline of Prayer," May 2002
N. Eldon Tanner, "Importance and Efficacy of Prayer," Aug. 1971
Spencer W. Kimball, "Pray Always," October 1981

NOTES:

Our Father in Heaven has promised us **peace** in times of trial and has provided a way for us to come to Him in our **need**. He has given us the privilege and power of

prayer.

—Rex D. Pinegar

Our Father in Heaven has promised us **peace** in times of trial and has provided a way for us to come to Him in our **need**. He has given us the privilege and power of

prayer.

—Rex D. Pinegar

Our Father in Heaven has promised us **peace** in times of trial and has provided a way for us to come to Him in our **need**. He has given us the privilege and power of

prayer.

—Rex D. Pinegar

Our Father in Heaven has promised us **peace** in times of trial and has provided a way for us to come to Him in our **need**. He has given us the privilege and power of

prayer.

—Rex D. Pinegar

LESSON NINE

PROPHETS OF GOD

Hymns

"Come, Listen to a Prophet's Voice — Hymns #21
"Come, Sing to the Lord" — Hymns #10
"God Bless Our Prophet Dear" — Hymns #24
"Praise to the Man" — Hymns #27
"We Thank Thee, O God, for a Prophet" — Hymns #19

SUMMARY:

God communicates to His people through a living prophet, a man called through priesthood authority to represent Him. The prophet is also the President of the Church of Jesus Christ of Latter-day Saints and holds the keys of the kingdom on Earth. The prophet receives revelation for the Church and leads the administration of priesthood ordinances. He is also called a seer and revelator. By following the Lord's chosen mouthpiece we will never be led astray.

QUOTES:

❧ "A prophet . . . is the authorized representative of the Lord. While the world may not recognize him, the important requirement is that God speaks through him" (A. Theodore Tuttle, "What Is a

Living Prophet?" *Ensign*, July 1973, 18–20).

ᴥ "Sustaining support of prophets, seers, and revelators is not in the upraised hand alone, but more so in our courage, testimony, and faith to listen to, heed, and follow them" (Dennis B. Neuenschwander, "Living Prophets, Seers, and Revelators," *Ensign*, Nov. 2000, 40–42).

ᴥ "When we sustain, it means we *do* something about our belief. Our testimony of the prophet turns into action when we sustain him" (Janette Hales Beckham, "Sustaining the Living Prophets," *Ensign*, May 1996, 84–85).

GOSPEL ART:

Building the Ark – 102
Noah and the Ark with Animals – 103
Abraham Taking Isaac to be Sacrificed – 105
Moses and the Burning Bush – 107
Moses Calls Aaron to the Ministry – 108
Boy Samuel Called by the Lord – 111
Enoch and His People Are Taken Up to God – 120
Lehi Prophesying to the People of Jerusalem – 300
Nephi Subdues His Rebellious Brothers – 303
Enos Praying – 305
Mormon Abridging the Plates – 306
King Benjamin Addresses His People – 307
Abinadi before King Noah – 308
Samuel the Lamanite on the Wall – 314
Mormon Bids Farewell to a Once Great Nation – 319
The Prophet Joseph Smith – 401
Latter-day Prophets – 506
Brigham Young – 507
John Taylor – 508

OBJECT LESSONS:

- Show the class a coin and tell them one side represents modern prophets and the other side ancient prophets. Ask them which side of the coin is more important. Then ask if the two sides of the coin can be separated. Explain that both sides of the coin work together for the same purpose, just as all prophets throughout the ages have had the common goal of bringing their people to Jesus Christ.

- Gift wrap two boxes. Leave one empty, but put some treats in the other one. Tell the class that one of the boxes has something special in it, while the other one has nothing. Ask a volunteer to choose a box. Let the volunteer see what's inside the box and ask the class if they want her to decide for them. Of course they'll say yes, because she now knows what's in both boxes. We follow the prophet because he has "seen what's in the box" of life! He knows what choices we need to make in order to receive eternal rewards.

❧ Hold a peanut with the shell in your hand behind your back and tell the class that you're holding something that has never been seen by human eyes before. Of course, they won't believe you. Ask for some volunteers to take a peek and tell the class if what you're saying is true. When they testify that you're telling the truth, ask how many believe now that there are witnesses. Some still won't. (They must be nuts.) Talk about how the prophets have "seen" and testify of truth. Some in the world will refuse to believe them . . . will you?

ENSIGN TALKS

F. Michael Watson, "His Servants, the Prophets," May 2009
David B. Haight, "A Prophet Chosen of the Lord," May 1986
Jeffrey R. Holland, "My Words . . . Never Cease," May 2008
Jeffrey R. Holland, "Prophets in the Land Again," Nov. 2006
Dieter F. Uchtdorf, "Heeding the Voice of the Prophets," July 2008
Gordon B. Hinckley, "We Thank Thee, O God, for a Prophet," Sept. 1991

NOTES:

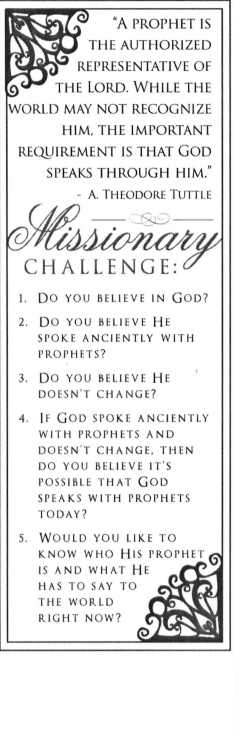

"A PROPHET IS THE AUTHORIZED REPRESENTATIVE OF THE LORD. WHILE THE WORLD MAY NOT RECOGNIZE HIM, THE IMPORTANT REQUIREMENT IS THAT GOD SPEAKS THROUGH HIM."

- A. THEODORE TUTTLE

Missionary
CHALLENGE:

1. DO YOU BELIEVE IN GOD?

2. DO YOU BELIEVE HE SPOKE ANCIENTLY WITH PROPHETS?

3. DO YOU BELIEVE HE DOESN'T CHANGE?

4. IF GOD SPOKE ANCIENTLY WITH PROPHETS AND DOESN'T CHANGE, THEN DO YOU BELIEVE IT'S POSSIBLE THAT GOD SPEAKS WITH PROPHETS TODAY?

5. WOULD YOU LIKE TO KNOW WHO HIS PROPHET IS AND WHAT HE HAS TO SAY TO THE WORLD RIGHT NOW?

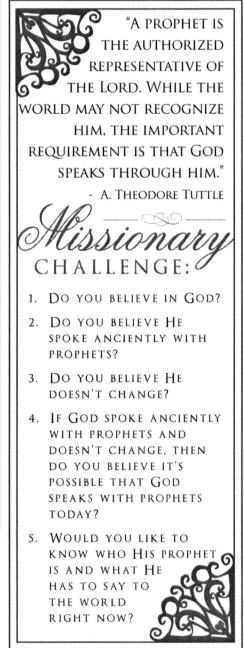

"A PROPHET IS THE AUTHORIZED REPRESENTATIVE OF THE LORD. WHILE THE WORLD MAY NOT RECOGNIZE HIM, THE IMPORTANT REQUIREMENT IS THAT GOD SPEAKS THROUGH HIM."

- A. THEODORE TUTTLE

Missionary
CHALLENGE:

1. DO YOU BELIEVE IN GOD?

2. DO YOU BELIEVE HE SPOKE ANCIENTLY WITH PROPHETS?

3. DO YOU BELIEVE HE DOESN'T CHANGE?

4. IF GOD SPOKE ANCIENTLY WITH PROPHETS AND DOESN'T CHANGE, THEN DO YOU BELIEVE IT'S POSSIBLE THAT GOD SPEAKS WITH PROPHETS TODAY?

5. WOULD YOU LIKE TO KNOW WHO HIS PROPHET IS AND WHAT HE HAS TO SAY TO THE WORLD RIGHT NOW?

LESSON TEN

SCRIPTURES

Hymns

"An Angel from on High" — Hymns #13
"As I Search the Holy Scriptures" — Hymns #277
"From Homes of Saints Glad Songs Arise" — Hymns #297
"Search, Ponder, and Pray" — Children's Songbook #109

SUMMARY:

Scriptures are sacred writings by the Lord's servants intended to reveal His plan for us and increase our understanding of Him. All scriptures testify of Jesus Christ and are designed to bring us closer to Him. The Church of Jesus Christ of Latter-day Saints accepts the following books as holy writ: the Bible, the Book of Mormon, the Doctrine and Covenants, and the Pearl of Great Price. The words from living prophets are also considered scripture. We are commanded to search and study the scriptures, and by doing so we will draw closer to the Savior.

QUOTES:

- "Through reading the scriptures, we can gain the assurance of the Spirit that that which we read has come of God for the enlightenment, blessing, and joy of His children" (Gordon B.

Hinckley, "Feasting upon the Scriptures," *Ensign*, Dec. 1985, 42–45).

⁊ "The holy scriptures are like letters from home telling us how we can draw near to our Father in Heaven" (Ardeth G. Kapp, "The Holy Scriptures: Letters from Home," *Ensign*, Nov. 1985, 93–95).

⁊ "Each of us, at some time in our lives, must discover the scriptures for ourselves—and not just discover them once, but rediscover them again and again" (Spencer W. Kimball, "How Rare a Possession—the Scriptures!" *Ensign*, Sept. 1976, 2–5).

⁊ "If you have not already developed the habit of daily scripture study, start now and keep studying in order to be prepared for your responsibilities in this life and in the eternities" (Julie B. Beck, "My Soul Delighteth in the Scriptures," *Ensign*, May 2004, 107–9).

⁊ "As a person studies the words of the Lord and obeys them, he or she draws closer to the Savior and obtains a greater desire to live a righteous life" (Merrill J. Bateman, "Coming unto Christ by Searching the Scriptures," *Ensign*, Nov. 1992, 27–28).

GOSPEL ART:

Moses and the Burning Bush – 107
Isaiah Writes of Christ's Birth – 113
Boy Jesus in the Temple – 205
The Liahona – 302
Mormon Abridging the Plates – 306
Moroni Hides the Plates in the Hill Cumorah – 320
Christ Asks for the Records – 323
The Gold Plates – 325
The Bible and Book of Mormon: Two Witnesses – 326

OBJECT LESSONS:

- Bring a plate of cookies and ask for volunteers to demonstrate different styles of eating: abstain, sample, taste, snack, gorge, nibble, eat, and feast. Now compare those styles to how we study the scriptures, reminding the class that we should "feast upon the words of Christ" (2 Nephi 32:3).

- Show the class two pictures that seem very much alike but have a few differences. Have the class point out the differences. In order to align our life with the Lord's will we need to follow His example. In order to discover the differences, we need to study the scriptures and change our life to match their model for us.

- Ask a class member to play a hymn on the harmonica. (Pick someone who doesn't know how to play it.) When they explain that they can't do it, ask them how they could learn. The answer is to study a manual or learn from someone who can. The same applies to learning to be like Heavenly Father; we can learn about Him in the scriptures and we can follow the Savior, who is like Him. Daily practice makes perfect!

ENSIGN TALKS

M. Russell Ballard, "The Miracle of the Holy Bible," May 2007

Ezra Taft Benson, "The Book of Mormon is the Word of God," Jan. 1988

Ezra Taft Benson, "The Book of Mormon and the Doctrine and Covenants," May 1987

Daniel C. Peterson, "Mounting Evidence for the Book of Mormon," Jan. 2000

L. Tom Perry, "Give Heed Unto the Word of the Lord," May 2000

Henry B. Eyring, "A Discussion on Scripture Study," July 2005

Lenet H. Read, "How the Bible Came to Be, parts 1–8" Jan.–Sept. 1982

Dallin H. Oaks, "Scripture Reading and Revelation," Jan.1995

NOTES:

My goal this week for scripture study is:

_____

_____

_____

_____

_____

"Each of us, at some time in our lives, must discover
the scriptures for ourselves—and not just discover
them once, but rediscover them again and again."
—Spencer W. Kimball

My goal this week for scripture study is:

_____

_____

_____

_____

_____

"Each of us, at some time in our lives, must discover
the scriptures for ourselves—and not just discover
them once, but rediscover them again and again."
—Spencer W. Kimball

LESSON ELEVEN

THE LIFE OF CHRIST

Hymns

"*I Believe in Christ*" — Hymns #134
" *'Tis Sweet To Sing the Matchless Love*" — Hymns #177

SUMMARY:

Jesus Christ's atoning sacrifice is the only way we can return to live with our Heavenly Father. He was born a poor infant under humble circumstances, but He is the creator of this Earth and will reign as its king in glory upon His return. Prophets in every dispensation understood His crucial role in the plan of happiness and have testified of His coming in holy scripture. By studying the scriptures we can learn how to love and serve more like Him. While on Earth, the Savior organized His church, showed us how to live, and saved us from physical and spiritual death through His redeeming Atonement.

QUOTES:

> "Each of [us] has the responsibility to know the Lord, love Him, follow Him, serve Him, and teach and testify of Him" (Russell

M. Nelson, "Jesus the Christ: Our Master and More," *Ensign*, Apr. 2000, 4–17; or *Liahona*, Apr. 2000, 4–19).

❧ "The soul that comes unto Christ dwells within a personal fortress, a veritable palace of perfect peace" (Jeffrey R. Holland, " 'Come unto Me,' " *Ensign*, Apr. 1998, 16–23).

❧ "He who is our Great Redeemer was fully qualified to become such, because He was and is the Great Emulator! We, in turn, have been asked to emulate Him" (Neal A. Maxwell, "Jesus, the Perfect Mentor," *Ensign*, Feb. 2001, 8–17).

❧ "The living water of Jesus is sure and certain to those who find Him and trust Him" (M. Russell Ballard, "Coming to Know Christ," *Ensign*, July 2001, 65).

GOSPEL ART:

OBJECT LESSONS

- Give everyone a bottle of water and ask them to talk about how Jesus Christ is like living water.

- Give a volunteer a compass and have her show the class where north is. Now turn her in a circle and point her in a different direction, asking her again to tell the class where north is. Jesus is like a compass—wherever we are He can point us in the right path.

ENSIGN TALKS:

Boyd K. Packer, "Who is Jesus Christ?" Mar. 2008

Gilbert W. Scharffs, "Unique Insights on Christ from the Book of Mormon," Dec. 1988

Jeffrey R. Holland, "Come Unto Me," Apr. 1998

David B. Haight, "Jesus of Nazareth," May 1994

Jay M. Todd, "The Life of Christ: Painted by Carl Heinrich Bloch," Jan. 1991

Monte S. Nyman, "I Am Jesus Christ the Son of God," Dec. 1999

Ray L. Huntington and Camille Fronk, "Latter-day Clarity on Christ's Life and Teachings," Jan. 1999

"A Chronology of the Life of Christ," Sept. 1974

Keith H. Pryor, "The Greatest Story Ever Foretold," Dec. 1991

NOTES:

"THE GIVING OF **GIFTS** IS NOT SOMETHING MAN INVENTED. GOD STARTED THE GIVING SPREE WHEN HE GAVE A **GIFT** BEYOND WORDS, THE UNSPEAKABLE GIFT OF **HIS SON**."

—ROBERT PLATT

"THE GIVING OF **GIFTS** IS NOT SOMETHING MAN INVENTED. GOD STARTED THE GIVING SPREE WHEN HE GAVE A **GIFT** BEYOND WORDS, THE UNSPEAKABLE GIFT OF **HIS SON**."

—ROBERT PLATT

"THE GIVING OF **GIFTS** IS NOT SOMETHING MAN INVENTED. GOD STARTED THE GIVING SPREE WHEN HE GAVE A **GIFT** BEYOND WORDS, THE UNSPEAKABLE GIFT OF **HIS SON**."

—ROBERT PLATT

"THE GIVING OF **GIFTS** IS NOT SOMETHING MAN INVENTED. GOD STARTED THE GIVING SPREE WHEN HE GAVE A **GIFT** BEYOND WORDS, THE UNSPEAKABLE GIFT OF **HIS SON**."

—ROBERT PLATT

"THE GIVING OF **GIFTS** IS NOT SOMETHING MAN INVENTED. GOD STARTED THE GIVING SPREE WHEN HE GAVE A **GIFT** BEYOND WORDS, THE UNSPEAKABLE GIFT OF **HIS SON**."

—ROBERT PLATT

"THE GIVING OF **GIFTS** IS NOT SOMETHING MAN INVENTED. GOD STARTED THE GIVING SPREE WHEN HE GAVE A **GIFT** BEYOND WORDS, THE UNSPEAKABLE GIFT OF **HIS SON**."

—ROBERT PLATT

"THE GIVING OF **GIFTS** IS NOT SOMETHING MAN INVENTED. GOD STARTED THE GIVING SPREE WHEN HE GAVE A **GIFT** BEYOND WORDS, THE UNSPEAKABLE GIFT OF **HIS SON**."

—ROBERT PLATT

"THE GIVING OF **GIFTS** IS NOT SOMETHING MAN INVENTED. GOD STARTED THE GIVING SPREE WHEN HE GAVE A **GIFT** BEYOND WORDS, THE UNSPEAKABLE GIFT OF **HIS SON**."

—ROBERT PLATT

"THE GIVING OF **GIFTS** IS NOT SOMETHING MAN INVENTED. GOD STARTED THE GIVING SPREE WHEN HE GAVE A **GIFT** BEYOND WORDS, THE UNSPEAKABLE GIFT OF **HIS SON**."

—ROBERT PLATT

LESSON TWELVE

THE ATONEMENT

Hymns

"Again We Meet around the Board" — Hymns #186
"Behold the Great Redeemer Die" — Hymns #191
"In Humility, Our Savior" — Hymns #172
"Our Savior's Love" — Hymns #113
"Rock of Ages" — Hymns #111
"Upon the Cross of Calvary" — Hymns #184

SUMMARY:

The most important event in the history of mankind was when the Savior was crucified for the world. Jesus Christ's Atonement took place in the Garden of Gethsemane and on the cross at Calvary. His redeeming sacrifice was necessary to ransom all people from the physical and spiritual effects of the Fall. Because of His merciful gift, everyone has the opportunity to repent, be forgiven of their sins, and be resurrected. The Savior was the only one capable of making a perfect atonement for all humankind because He is the only son of God in the flesh, He was completely obedient, and was without sin. To thank Him for paying our spiritual and physical debts, we must show faith in Him, repent of our sins, be baptized, and follow Him.

QUOTES:

- "If we could truly understand the Atonement of the Lord Jesus Christ, we would realize how precious is *one* son or daughter of God" (M. Russell Ballard, "The Atonement and the Value of One Soul," *Ensign*, May 2004, 84–87).

- "Faith in the Savior's resurrection should help us carry all burdens, bear any sorrows, and also fully savor all joys and happiness that can be found in this life" (James E. Faust, "The Supernal Gift of the Atonement," *Ensign*, Nov. 1988, 12–14).

- "[The Lord's] atonement is the most transcendent event that ever has or ever will occur, from Creation's dawn through all the ages of a never-ending eternity" (Bruce R. McConkie, "The Purifying Power of Gethsemane," *Ensign*, May 1985, 9–11).

GOSPEL ART:

An Angel Saves Abraham – 104
Abraham Taking Isaac to Be Sacrificed – 105
Triumphal Entry – 223
Jesus Washing the Apostles' Feet – 226
Jesus Praying in Gethsemane – 227
The Betrayal of Jesus – 228
The Crucifixion – 230
Jesus' Tomb – 232
Mary and the Resurrected Lord – 233
Jesus Shows His Wounds – 234
The Ascension of Jesus – 236
The Second Coming – 238
The Resurrected Jesus Christ – 239
The Empty Tomb – 245

OBJECT LESSONS:

- Ask someone in the class to put on a sock. Hand the volunteer a muddy sock. The volunteer will probably not want to touch the dirty sock, so ask her what could be done to make her willing. Tell her you'll take the muddy sock and give her a clean, new one. The Savior took upon Himself all of our dirty sins and gave us each a clean sock to wear when we return to our Father in Heaven so that we will be clean from the sins of the world.

- Pass around a beautiful rose that has thorns still intact. Talk about how fragrant and pleasing it is. Next, bruise some of the rose petals and point out the thorns. Jesus' body was bruised for our iniquities and a crown of thorns was placed on his head. Now ask someone to be a timekeeper and someone else to take the rose petals off the stem as fast as possible. Ask for another volunteer and timekeeper. Say, "Okay, see if you can beat that time. Ready? Put it back together!" No matter how hard we try, we can't rebuild a rose, but God can not only do that, but He can also restore life through Jesus Christ. Everyone will be resurrected. With God, all things are possible!

- Ask for a volunteer to stand in a square that is marked on the floor with masking tape. Show her a candy bar on the table and tell her she can have it only if she can reach it without leaving the square. After she gives her best effort, have her ask for another volunteer to help. That's what the Savior did for us—He gave us the sweet gift of eternal life!

ENSIGN TALKS:

M. Russell Ballard, "The Atonement and the Value of One Soul," May 2004

Cecil O. Samuelson Jr., "What Does the Atonement Mean to You?" Apr. 2009

Russell M. Nelson, "The Atonement," Nov. 1996

Marion G. Romney, "Christ's Atonement: The Gift Supreme," Dec. 1973

Shayne M. Bowen, "The Atonement Can Clean, Reclaim, and Sanctify Our Lives," Nov. 2006

James E. Faust, "The Atonement: Our Greatest Hope," Nov. 2001

David B. Haight, "Remembering the Savior's Atonement," Apr. 1988

NOTES:

"THE LORD'S ATONEMENT IS THE MOST

TRANSCENDENT EVENT THAT

EVER HAS OR EVER WILL

OCCUR, FROM CREATION'S DAWN THROUGH

ALL THE AGES OF A NEVER-ENDING ETERNITY."

—BRUCE R. McCONKIE

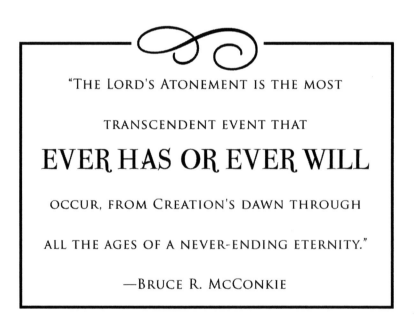

"THE LORD'S ATONEMENT IS THE MOST

TRANSCENDENT EVENT THAT

EVER HAS OR EVER WILL

OCCUR, FROM CREATION'S DAWN THROUGH

ALL THE AGES OF A NEVER-ENDING ETERNITY."

—BRUCE R. McCONKIE

LESSON THIRTEEN

THE PRIESTHOOD

Hymns

"*Ye Elders of Israel*" — Hymns 319
"*The Priesthood of Our Lord*" — Hymns #320
"*Come, All Ye Sons of God*" — Hymns #322
"*Rise Up, O Men of God*" — Hymns #323
"*See the Mighty Priesthood*" — Hymns #325

SUMMARY:

The priesthood is the power and authority of God given to righteous men to enable them to act in God's name for the salvation of the human family. Earthly ordinances, such as baptism, confirmation, administration of the sacrament, and temple marriage, need to be performed by the correct priesthood authority in order to be valid in the eyes of the Lord.

QUOTES:

     "When one becomes a holder of the priesthood, he becomes an agent of the Lord. He should think of his calling as though he were on the Lord's errand" (Harold B. Lee, as quoted by Thomas S. Monson, "To Learn, to Do, to Be," *Ensign*, Nov. 2008, 60–62, 67–68).

❧ "I like to define the Priesthood in terms of service and I frequently call it the perfect plan of service. I do so because it seems to me that it is only through the utilization of the divine power conferred on men that they may ever hope to realize the full import and vitality of this endowment" (Stephen L. Richards, as quoted by Thomas S. Monson, "To Learn, to Do, to Be," *Ensign*, Nov. 2008, 60–62, 67–68).

❧ "When we consider how few men who have lived on Earth have received the priesthood and how Jesus Christ has empowered those individuals to act in His name, we should feel deeply humble and profoundly grateful for the priesthood we hold" (Richard G. Scott, "Honor the Priesthood and Use it Well," *Ensign*, Nov. 2008, 44–47).

❧ "While the power *of* the priesthood is unlimited, our individual power *in* the priesthood is limited by our degree of righteousness or purity" (John H. Groberg, "Priesthood Power," *Ensign*, May 2001, 43–44; or *Liahona*, July 2001, 51–53).

❧ "Caring for others is the very essence of priesthood responsibility. It is the power to bless, to heal, and to administer the saving ordinances of the gospel" (James E. Faust, "Power of the Priesthood," *Ensign*, May 1997, 41–43).

GOSPEL ART:

Moses Calls Aaron to the Ministry – 108
Jacob Blessing His Sons – 122
Calling of the Fishermen – 209
Christ Ordaining the Apostles – 211
Christ Healing a Blind Man – 213
Stilling the Storm – 214
Jesus Blessing Jairus's Daughter – 215
Jesus Washing the Apostles' Feet – 226

Christ With the Three Disciples – 324
John the Baptist Conferring the Aaronic Priesthood – 407
Melchizedek Priesthood Restoration – 408
Baptism – 601
The Gift of the Holy Ghost – 602
Blessing the Sacrament – 603
Passing the Sacrament – 604
The Bishop – 611
Missionaries Teach the Gospel of Jesus Christ – 612
Administering to the Sick – 613
Home Teaching – 614

OBJECT LESSON:

- Take a "Master" lock and attach a sign to it that says "Eternal Life." The only way to get "Eternal Life" is if you unlock the lock. Give several keys to a class member and let her choose one while passing the rest to the person next to her. Have the class members continue taking a key and passing the rest on. Discuss how the keys of the priesthood are passed from one individual to another worthy individual. Once the keys are passed out, ask a person without a key to unlock the lock to gain eternal life. She will not be able to because she doesn't have a key. Then give the lock to the person that has the correct key. Discuss how ordinances need to be performed by the correct authority or else they will not be able to open the lock of eternal life.

- Ask someone in the class to hold an umbrella and keep someone in the class dry from the pretend rain that is falling. Note that the umbrella only needs to be held by one person, but both people are kept dry from the rain. So it is with the priesthood; while men can hold the priesthood, it is meant to be used to bless everyone and keep us all protected from the storms of earthly life.

ENSIGN TALKS:

Henry B. Eyring, "Faith and the Oath and Covenant of the Priesthood," May 2008

Thomas S. Monson, "Our Sacred Priesthood Trust," May 2006

Dallin H. Oaks, "Priesthood Blessings," May 1987

Thomas S. Monson, "The Priesthood—A Sacred Gift," May 2007

Russell M. Nelson, "Honoring the Priesthood," May 1993

NOTES:

THE AARONIC PRIESTHOOD

isn't a gift; it's an honor. It is a call to serve others.

— Thomas S. Monson

THE AARONIC PRIESTHOOD

isn't a gift; it's an honor. It is a call to serve others.

— Thomas S. Monson

THE AARONIC PRIESTHOOD

isn't a gift; it's an honor. It is a call to serve others.

— Thomas S. Monson

THE AARONIC PRIESTHOOD

isn't a gift; it's an honor. It is a call to serve others.

— Thomas S. Monson

PRIESTHOOD ORGANIZATION

Hymns

"Ye Elders of Israel" — Hymns 319
"The Priesthood of Our Lord" — Hymns #320
"Come, All Ye Sons of God" — Hymns #322
"Rise Up, O Men of God" — Hymns #323
"See the Mighty Priesthood" — Hymns #325

SUMMARY:

The priesthood is the power of God, given to righteous men to act for Him and administer His work on the Earth. The Melchizedek Priesthood is conferred on worthy men and includes the offices of Elder, High Priest, Patriarch, Seventy, and Apostle. The lesser priesthood, the Aaronic Priesthood, includes the offices of deacon, teacher, priest, and bishop. Boys and men are ordained to an office of the priesthood and placed in a quorum, performing specific duties and giving service to others.

QUOTES:

❧ "When ordained to an office in the priesthood, you are granted authority. But power comes from exercising that authority in righteousness" (Russell M. Nelson, "Personal Priesthood

Responsibility," *Ensign*, Nov. 2003, 44–47; or *Liahona*, Nov. 2003, 44–47).

ॐ "With the priesthood, nothing is impossible in carrying forward the work of the kingdom of God. . . . It is the only power on the earth that reaches beyond the veil of death" (Gordon B. Hinckley, "Priesthood Restoration," *Ensign*, Oct. 1988, 69–72).

ॐ "The priesthood of God gives light to His children in this dark and troubled world" (Robert D. Hales, "Blessings of the Priesthood," *Ensign*, Nov. 1995, 32–34).

GOSPEL ART:

Moses Calls Aaron to the Ministry – 108

Calling of the Fishermen – 209

Christ Ordaining the Apostles – 211

Jesus Washing the Apostles' Feet – 226

Christ with the Three Disciples - 324

John the Baptist Conferring the Aaronic Priesthood – 407

Melchizadek Priesthood Restoration – 408

Baptism – 601

The Gift of the Holy Ghost – 602

Blessing the Sacrament – 603

Passing the Sacrament – 604

Sustaining Our Leaders – 610

The Bishop – 611

Missionaries Teach the Gospel of Jesus Christ – 612

Administering the Sick – 613

Home Teaching – 614

Serving One Another – 615

OBJECT LESSONS

⁊ Before class, get a stalk of celery, freshly cut on one end. Place it in a glass half full of grape juice or red-dyed water. Show the class how the celery will soak up the color through its stem, thus changing the color of the celery. The glass of colored water represents the power of God. The stalk of celery represents a worthy man. When given the priesthood, the celery uses that same power as God, and in fact, is transformed by it.

⁊ Show the class a gyroscope. It's not just a toy, but a scientific instrument. To make it work, start it spinning and pull the string. If you put it on a tiny surface, it will still spin and stay upright. In fact, whatever the position it's placed in, it will continue to spin. The gyroscope principle is used in a special type of compass used on a ship because the movement won't affect it. There are many things that can knock us off course in life, but if we follow the leadership of the priesthood, our direction will always be right.

ENSIGN TALKS:

Henry B. Eyring, "God Helps the Faithful Priesthood Holder," Nov. 2007

Richard G. Scott, "Honor the Priesthood and Use It Well," Nov. 2008

Claudio R. M. Costa, "Priesthood Responsibilities," May 2009

Thomas S. Monson, "True To Our Priesthood Trust," Nov. 2006

James E. Faust, "A Royal Priesthood," May 2006, Nov. 2007

Thomas S. Monson, "The Call To Serve," Nov. 2000

Russell M. Nelson, "Personal Priesthood Responsibility," Nov. 2003

NOTES:

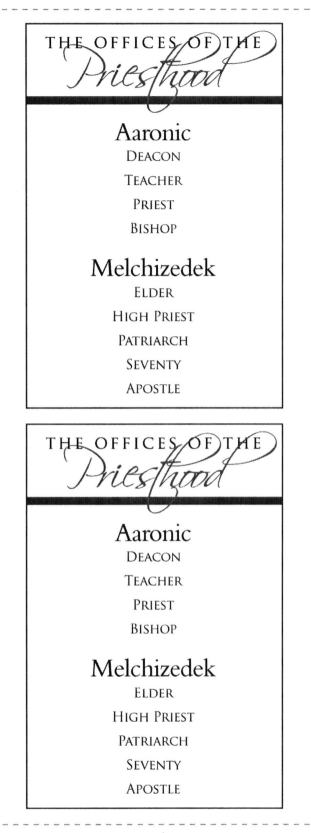

THE OFFICES OF THE

Priesthood

Aaronic

DEACON

TEACHER

PRIEST

BISHOP

Melchizedek

ELDER

HIGH PRIEST

PATRIARCH

SEVENTY

APOSTLE

THE OFFICES OF THE

Priesthood

Aaronic

DEACON

TEACHER

PRIEST

BISHOP

Melchizedek

ELDER

HIGH PRIEST

PATRIARCH

SEVENTY

APOSTLE

LESSON FIFTEEN

THE LORD'S COVENANT PEOPLE

Hymns

"I'll Go Where You Want Me to Go" — Hymns #270
"Let Us All Press On" — Hymns #243
"True to the Faith" — Hymns #254
"We Are All Enlisted" — Hymns #250
"Who's On the Lord's Side" — Hymns #260

SUMMARY:

From the very beginning of time, God has made covenants (promises) with His children. A covenant is a mutual agreement between God and an individual or group of people, where both parties make a sacred promise to perform certain things. God promises specific blessings when we obey certain commandments. He sets the terms of the covenant and we agree to obey. The Abrahamic covenant is an example of a covenant that extends certain blessings to us even today. The fulness of the gospel of Jesus Christ is called the new and everlasting covenant. The purpose of covenants is to bind us to the Lord. Membership in The Church of Jesus Christ of Latter-day Saints offers us many blessings as His covenant people, as well as responsibilities to fulfill our promises.

QUOTES:

ఞ "For members of this Church to enjoy the blessings of a covenant people, the law of the Lord must be written in their hearts" (James E. Faust, " 'Search Me, O God, and Know My Heart," *Ensign*, May 1998).

ఞ "Our honest effort to keep our covenants allows God to increase our power to do it" (Henry B. Eyring, "Witnesses for God," *Ensign*, Nov. 1996, 30–33).

ఞ "The covenants we enter into here in mortality are to help us attain our objective of eternal life, which is explained in, and made possible by, the new and everlasting covenant of the gospel" (Marion G. Romney, "According to the Covenants," *Ensign*, Nov. 1975, 71–73).

ఞ "Making covenants with his people and with individuals has always been one of the principal ways in which the Lord deals with them" (ElRay L. Christiansen, "We Have Made Covenants with the Lord," *Ensign*, Jan. 1973, 50–51).

ఞ "Father in Heaven knows us as individuals. The covenants we make with Him are performed one on one" (Bonnie D. Parkin, "Celebrating Covenants," *Ensign*, May 1995, 78–79).

GOSPEL ART:

An Angel Saves Abraham – 104
Abraham Taking Isaac to Be Sacrificed – 105
Moses and the Burning Bush – 107
Moses Calls Aaron to the Ministry – 108
Boy Samuel Called by the Lord – 111

Jacob Blessing His Sons – 122
Christ Ordaining the Apostles – 211
Jesus Washing the Apostles' Feet – 226
Lehi's Family Leaving Jerusalem – 301
Lehi and His People Arrive in the Promised Land – 304
King Benjamin Addresses His People – 307
Alma Baptizes in the Waters of Mormon – 309
Jesus Teaching in the Western Hemisphere – 316
Elijah Restores the Power to Seal Families for Eternity – 417
Apostle Orson Hyde Dedicates the Holy Land – 419
Pioneers Arrive by Ship in San Francisco Bay – 421
Kirtland Temple – 500
Nauvoo Illinois Temple – 501
Salt Lake Temple – 502
Temple Baptismal Font – 504

OBJECT LESSONS:

⁊ Display small bowls that contain various white powdery substances, such as baking soda, baking powder, pancake mix, flour, sugar, salt. In another bowl put some powdered lime that's used for the garden or powdered chalk. Tell the class that all of them but one came from the kitchen and are edible. Ask the class which ones are safe to eat. They probably won't be able to tell. Explain how some people say they are Christians, but unless they're truly following the Savior and making covenants with Him, the Lord will "spew them out of His mouth."

⁊ Bring a weasel ball (can be found at toy stores) and another ball. When turned on, the weasel ball goes all over the place by itself, while the other ball sits still. What kind of member are you? Lively or lifeless? Explain how the Lord's covenant people show who they are by their actions and willingness to do His will.

ᴥ Show a variety of tools: scale, ruler, measuring cups, spoons, thermometer, voltage detector, stop watch, carpenter's level, and so forth. Ask the class what all of the things have in common. They are all used to measure things. Ask how we measure true discipleship. Explain how the Lord's true followers make covenants with Him to show their dedication and love.

ᴥ Hand someone in the class a pencil and ask them to "try to drop it." When the person drops it, say "No, I said to *try* to drop it." Have them keep "trying" until they finally catch on that they're really not supposed to drop it. Explain to the class that there is no *try*—either you do it or you don't. The Lord's covenant people *do*.

ENSIGN TALKS:

Dennis B. Neuenschwander, "Ordinances and Covenants," Aug. 2001
M. Russell Ballard, "Keeping Covenants," May 1993
D. Todd Christofferson, "The Power of Covenants," May 2009
Russell M. Nelson, "The Gathering of Scattered Israel," Nov. 2006
Russell M. Nelson, "Children of the Covenant," May 1995
Lance B. Wickman, "Of Compasses and Covenants," June 1996
Paul K. Browning, "Gathering Scattered Israel: Then and Now," July 1998

NOTES:

FOR MEMBERS OF THIS CHURCH
to enjoy the *blessings* of a covenant people, the
law of the Lord must be written in their *hearts.*
—James E. Faust

FOR MEMBERS OF THIS CHURCH
to enjoy the *blessings* of a covenant people, the
law of the Lord must be written in their *hearts.*
—James E. Faust

FOR MEMBERS OF THIS CHURCH
to enjoy the *blessings* of a covenant people, the
law of the Lord must be written in their *hearts.*
—James E. Faust

FOR MEMBERS OF THIS CHURCH
to enjoy the *blessings* of a covenant people, the
law of the Lord must be written in their *hearts.*
—James E. Faust

THE CHURCH OF JESUS CHRIST IN FORMER TIMES

Hymns

"For All the Saints" – Hymns #82
"Faith of our Fathers" – Hymns #84
"God of Our Fathers, Known of Old" – Hymns #80
"Gof of Our Fathers, We Come unto Thee" – Hymns #76
"Israel, Israel, God is Calling" – Hymns #7

SUMMARY:

When Jesus Christ was on Earth, He established His Church, giving priesthood authority to the Twelve Apostles to lead His Church in His absence. The first principles and ordinances of the gospel are faith in Jesus Christ, repentance, and baptism. Priesthood keys and eternal truths were lost during the Great Apostasy; however, the fullness of the gospel and Christ's Church were restored in the latter-days by a living prophet.

QUOTES:

❧ "The organization is now in place to keep the administration of the Church close to the prophets, seers, and revelators whom the Lord has called to direct the work" (L. Aldin Porter, "A History of the Latter-day Seventy," *Ensign*, Aug. 2000, 14–20).

    "All divine powers of previous dispensations were to be restored. This dispensation of the fulness of times would not be limited in time or in location. It would not end in apostasy, and it would fill the world" (Russell M. Nelson, "The Gathering of Scattered Israel," *Ensign*, Nov. 2006, 79–82).

    "The doctrine of the Restoration is glorious in and of itself, but the thing that makes it powerful and imbues it with great meaning is the personal testimonies of Church members worldwide who accept the Restoration of the gospel and strive to live its teachings every day of their lives. . . . It also brings a confirmation to our soul of the Restoration of the gospel in these latter days" (M. Russell Ballard, "Pure Testimony," *Ensign*, Nov. 2004, 40–43).

GOSPEL ART:

Temple Used Anciently – 118
Boy Jesus in the Temple – 205
John the Baptist Baptizing Jesus – 208
Calling of the Fishermen – 209
Christ Ordaining the Apostles – 211
Sermon on the Mount – 212
Christ Healing a Blind Man – 213
Stilling the Storm – 214
Jesus Blessing Jairus's Daughter – 215
Christ and the Children – 216
Triumphal Entry – 223
Jesus Washing the Apostles' Feet – 226
Jesus Shows His Wounds – 234
Go Ye Therefore – 235
King Benjamin Addresses His People – 307
Alma Baptizes in the Waters of Mormon – 309

OBJECT LESSONS:

- Show a light bulb that has words written on it with a marker, such as baptism, priesthood, Godhead, temples, and so forth. Talk about the gospel truths Christ taught when He was here on Earth. Attach twelve long strings or ribbons to the bulb and explain that they represent the Twelve Apostles who were chosen by Jesus Christ to lead His church in the meridian of time. Turn the light off, which represents when Christ ascended into heaven, leaving the apostles to lead the church. Pull the strings off the bulb as you talk about how they were killed and how the early Church struggled in their absence. Explain that if you were to drop the bulb it would shatter into fragments, which is what happened to the church and its truths. When Joseph Smith prayed in the Sacred Grove, it was like turning on the light again!

- Invite the class to take a half sheet of paper and put a dark black line about 2 inches long followed by an X then another 2 inches long line followed by an O then another 2 inches long line. It should look something like this:

    _____X _____O _____

    Tell them to close their right eye and look at the circle on the right with their left eye. Tell them to move the paper back and forth in front of their faces approximately 5–10 inches from their eyes until the X disappears. Each eye has a blind spot where the optic nerve is located. Our minds fill in the blank spot with what seems logical. The X represents when the apostles had Christ with them to lead the church. The O represents when they tried to continue leading the church and remembered what He had taught them.

ENSIGN TALKS:

S. Kent Brown, "Whither the Early Church?" Oct. 1988

Kent P. Jackson, "Early Signs of the Apostasy," Dec. 1984

Richard Lloyd Anderson, "The Church and the Roman Empire," Sept. 1975

H. Ross Workman, "Words of the Early Apostles: Safely Anchored by Love," Dec. 2003

Andrew C. Skinner, "Apostasy, Restoration, and Lessons in Faith," Dec. 1995

James E. Faust, "The Restoration of All Things," May 2006

Marion G. Romney, "Why the Church of Jesus Christ of Latter-day Saints," Jan. 1973

M. Russell Ballard, "How Is It With Us?" May 2000

NOTES:

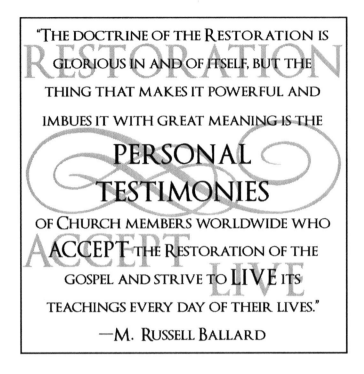

"The doctrine of the Restoration is glorious in and of itself, but the thing that makes it powerful and imbues it with great meaning is the **PERSONAL TESTIMONIES** of Church members worldwide who ACCEPT the Restoration of the gospel and strive to LIVE its teachings every day of their lives."

—M. Russell Ballard

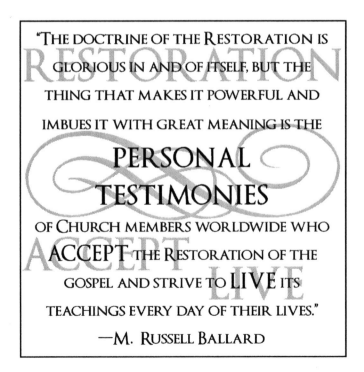

"The doctrine of the Restoration is glorious in and of itself, but the thing that makes it powerful and imbues it with great meaning is the **PERSONAL TESTIMONIES** of Church members worldwide who ACCEPT the Restoration of the gospel and strive to LIVE its teachings every day of their lives."

—M. Russell Ballard

LESSON SEVENTEEN

THE CHURCH OF JESUS CHRIST TODAY

Hymns

"Come, Rejoice" — *Hymns #9*
"Great Is the Lord" — *Hymns #77*
"The Glorious Gospel Light Has Shone" — *Hymns #283*
"Twas Witnessed in the Morning Sky" — *Hymns #12*
"Come, All Ye Sons of God" — *Hymns #322*
"Behold a Royal Army" — *Hymns #251*
"High on the Mountain Top" — *Hymns #5*

SUMMARY:

After the Savior ascended into heaven, His Church and its ordinances and teachings were lost in their purity. Priesthood authority and correct doctrine were restored in 1830, when a prophet of God was again chosen. The Church of Jesus Christ of Latter-day Saints offers the fulness of the gospel to the world today and will never be destroyed.

QUOTES:

- "The Church is no bigger than a ward. . . . Everything needed for our redemption, save for the temple, is centered there—and temples now come ever closer to all of us" (Boyd K. Packer, "The Bishop and His Counselors," *Ensign*, May 1999, 57–63).

- "We declare to the world that the fulness of the gospel of Jesus Christ has been restored to the earth" (L. Tom Perry, "The

Message of the Restoration," *Ensign*, May 2007, 85–88).

ᴥ "The dawn of the dispensation of the fulness of times rose upon the world. All of the good, the beautiful, the divine of all previous dispensations was restored in this most remarkable season" (Gordon B. Hinckley, "The Dawning of a Brighter Day," *Ensign*, May 2004, 83).

GOSPEL ART:

Daniel Interprets Nebuchadnezzar's Dream – 115
The Bible and Book of Mormon: Two Witnesses – 326
Mary Fielding and Joseph F. Smith Crossing the Plains – 412
Martin Handcart Company—Bitter Creek, Wyoming, 1856 – 414
Helping the Martin Handcart Company across the Sweetwater River – 415
Four Missionaries to the Lamanites – 418
Apostle Orson Hyde Dedicates the Holy Land – 419
Pioneers Arrive by Ship in San Francisco Bay – 421
Kirtland Temple – 500
Nauvoo Illinois Temple – 501
Salt Lake Temple – 502
Salt Lake Tabernacle – 503
Temple Baptismal Font – 504
Washington DC Temple – 505
Latter-day Prophets – 506
Brigham Young – 507
John Taylor – 508
Wilford Woodruff – 509
Lorenzo Snow – 510
Joseph F. Smith – 511
Heber J. Grant – 512
George Albert Smith – 513

OBJECT LESSONS:

❧ Pass out gum to the class and tell them to chew it for about 5 minutes to get all of the flavor out of it. Now ask the class to put it back into the wrapper and mold it into the original form. Explain how many men have tried to recreate Christ's true church. Only with the Savior's help was Joseph Smith able to restore the Lord's Church.

❧ Show the class some tarnished silver spoons. Talk about what the restoration was while you polish the silver. Discuss how the beauty was always there, but that no one could see it until it was restored.

ENSIGN TALKS:

Jeffrey R. Holland, "This, The Greatest of All Dispensations," July 2007

Russell M. Nelson, "Thus Shall My Church Be Called," May 1990

D. Todd Christofferson, "Come to Zion," Nov. 2008

Henry B. Eyring, "The True and Living Church," May 2008

M. Russell Ballard, "The Truth of God Shall Go Forth," Nov. 2008

NOTES:

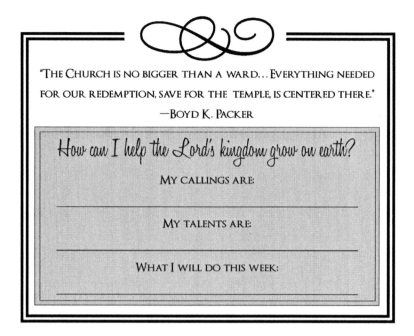

"THE CHURCH IS NO BIGGER THAN A WARD... EVERYTHING NEEDED FOR OUR REDEMPTION, SAVE FOR THE TEMPLE, IS CENTERED THERE."
—BOYD K. PACKER

How can I help the Lord's kingdom grow on earth?

MY CALLINGS ARE:

_____

MY TALENTS ARE:

_____

WHAT I WILL DO THIS WEEK:

_____

"THE CHURCH IS NO BIGGER THAN A WARD... EVERYTHING NEEDED FOR OUR REDEMPTION, SAVE FOR THE TEMPLE, IS CENTERED THERE."
—BOYD K. PACKER

How can I help the Lord's kingdom grow on earth?

MY CALLINGS ARE:

_____

MY TALENTS ARE:

_____

WHAT I WILL DO THIS WEEK:

_____

LESSON EIGHTEEN

FAITH IN JESUS CHRIST

Hymns

"Go Forth With Faith" — Hymns #263
"Come Unto Him" — Hymns #114
"Faith of Our Fathers" — Hymns #84
"Testimony" — Hymns #137
"When Faith Endures" — Hymns #128
"True to the Faith" — Hymns #254

SUMMARY:

The first principle of the gospel is faith in the Lord Jesus Christ. Faith is believing in Him with our spiritual eyes when we haven't seen Him with our physical eyes. It is a principle of action that compels us to pray, be obedient, and trust in His promises. We increase our faith by testing and studying His words. Faith has power to move mountains, perform miracles, and prove us worthy to see God.

QUOTES:

❧ "Only faith in the Lord Jesus Christ and His Atonement can bring us peace, hope, and understanding" (Robert D. Hales, "Finding Faith in the Lord Jesus Christ," *Ensign*, Nov. 2004, 70–73; or *Liahona*, Nov. 2004, 70–73).

ક⋗ "We promote the process of strengthening our faith when we do what is right—increased faith always follows" (L. Whitney Clayton, " 'Help Thou Mine Unbelief,' " *Ensign*, Nov. 2001, 28–29).

ક⋗ "Faith in Jesus Christ takes us beyond mere acceptance of the Savior's identity and existence. It includes having complete confidence in His infinite and eternal redemptive power" (James O. Mason, "Faith in Jesus Christ," *Ensign*, Apr. 2001, 22–27).

ક⋗ "Faith in the Lord Jesus Christ is a conviction and trust that God knows us and loves us and will hear our prayers and answer them with what is best for us" (Dallin H. Oaks, "Faith in the Lord Jesus Christ," *Ensign*, May 1994, 98–100).

GOSPEL ART:

Abraham Taking Isaac to Be Sacrificed – 105
Three Men in the Fiery Furnace – 116
Daniel in the Lions' Den – 117
Moses and the Brass Serpent – 123
Christ Healing a Blind Man – 213
Jesus Blessing Jairus's Daughter – 215
Christ and the Children – 216
The Liahona – 302
The Anti-Nephi-Lehies Burying Their Swords – 311
Two Thousand Young Warriors – 313
The Brother of Jared Sees the Finger of the Lord – 318
Mary Fielding and Joseph F. Smith Crossing the Plains – 412
Martin Handcart Company—Bitter Creek, Wyoming, 1856 – 414
Helping the Martin Handcart Company across the Sweetwater River – 415
Christ and Children From Around the World – 608
The Articles of Faith – 618

OBJECT LESSONS

❧ Pass out some baby food jars filled with unwhipped whipping cream. Ask the class if they have faith that the cream can turn into butter. Explain that faith isn't just believing in something, it also leads to action. Have the class shake the jars during the lesson until the cream turns into sweet butter. Talk about how faith requires patience and waiting because we often don't see the reward until much later. Before the lesson ends pass out blueberry muffins that the butter can be served on for all to enjoy.

❧ Hand each person in class a clear marble and ask them to look through it. The image of whatever they're looking at will be upside down. Share Romans 12:2. Explain how in today's world where society calls good evil and evil good, we can have faith that when Christ comes again, all will be transformed to that which is right. Having faith in Jesus Christ helps us see correctly with our spiritual eyes.

❧ Show the class a checkerboard with 1 grain of wheat on the first square, 2 on the second, 4 on the third, and 8, 16, 32, 64, 128, and so forth. Ask the class, "At this rate of doubling every square, how much grain would you have on the checkerboard by the time you reach the 64th square?" Let the class guess and tell them the correct answer is enough grain to cover the entire subcontinent of India 50 feet deep! Each square represents some area of their life where they need to trust God. Talk about how our faith may start out small, but as God uses it, the end result can be miraculous and quite powerful!

ENSIGN TALKS:

Gordon B. Hinckley, "Faith: The Essence of True Religion," Oct. 1995
Russell M. Nelson, "Faith in Jesus Christ," Mar. 2008
Kevin W. Pearson, "Faith in the Lord Jesus Christ," May 2009
Gordon B. Hinckley, "The Cornerstones of Our Faith," Nov. 1984
Robert D. Hales, "Finding Faith in the Lord Jesus Christ," Nov. 2004
Gordon B. Hinckley, "Be Not Faithless," Apr. 1989
Quentin L. Cook, "Live By Faith and Not by Fear," Nov. 2007

NOTES:

FAITH IN THE LORD JESUS CHRIST IS A CONVICTION AND TRUST THAT GOD KNOWS US AND LOVES US AND WILL HEAR OUR PRAYERS AND ANSWER THEM WITH WHAT IS BEST FOR US.

—DALLIN H. OAKS

FAITH IN THE LORD JESUS CHRIST IS A CONVICTION AND TRUST THAT GOD KNOWS US AND LOVES US AND WILL HEAR OUR PRAYERS AND ANSWER THEM WITH WHAT IS BEST FOR US.

—DALLIN H. OAKS

FAITH IN THE LORD JESUS CHRIST IS A CONVICTION AND TRUST THAT GOD KNOWS US AND LOVES US AND WILL HEAR OUR PRAYERS AND ANSWER THEM WITH WHAT IS BEST FOR US.

—DALLIN H. OAKS

LESSON NINETEEN

REPENTANCE

Hymns

"With Humble Heart" — Hymns #171
"Savior, Redeemer of My Soul" — Hymns #112
"Come unto Jesus" — Hymns #117
"Come, Ye Disconsolate" — Hymns #115

SUMMARY:

We all sin when we are less than perfect in our obedience to God's laws. Only Jesus Christ was without sin. A merciful Father in Heaven sent His Son to atone for our sins so that we may return to His presence. Repentance is the process that allows us to receive forgiveness and grow spiritually. The steps of repentance include recognizing our error, feeling sorrow for our sin, forsaking our bad behavior, confessing our sins (to the Lord, or for more serious sins, to the Lord's servant), and making restitution to right the wrong. We are also commanded to forgive others and to not procrastinate our repentance.

QUOTES:

» "The promise of the Lord is that He will cleanse our garments with His blood. . . . He can redeem us from our personal fall"

(Lynn A. Mickelsen, "The Atonement, Repentance, and Dirty Linen," *Ensign*, Nov. 2003, 10–13).

ભ "The steps of repentance . . . produce purity, peace of mind, self-respect, hope, and finally, a new person with a renewed life and abundance of opportunity" (Richard G. Scott, "Finding Forgiveness," *Ensign*, May 1995, 75–77).

ભ "Repentance is timeless. The evidence of repentance is transformation" (Spencer W. Kimball, "What Is True Repentance?" *New Era*, May 1974, 4–7)

GOSPEL ART:

The Prodigal Son – 220
Jesus Praying in Gethsemane – 227
The Crucifixion – 230
Jesus at the Door – 237
The Resurrected Jesus Christ – 239
Jesus the Christ – 240
Enos Praying – 305
The Anti-Nephi-Lehies Burying Their Swords – 311
Conversion of Alma the Younger – 321

OBJECT LESSONS:

ભ Hand out various objects to class members and have them explain how those items are like repentance. Easy objects to use include:
— soap
— pencil eraser
— knotted rope
— calculator

⁊ Start with a jar filled with clear water and label it US. Next, take food coloring, labeled SIN and add a drop each time you discuss various sins. Talk about the Atonement as you pour some bleach, labeled ATONEMENT, into the jar. Stir the water, which represents REPENTANCE and the class should see that the water clears up and is "clean" like before.

⁊ Wear a long-sleeved white buttoned-up shirt that has holes in it, dirt marks, food smears and words that say things like: drugs, profanity, gossip, anger, stealing, lying, disobedience, and so on. When you talk about repentance, take that shirt off, revealing a clean, white shirt underneath.

ENSIGN TALKS:

Spencer W. Kimball, "The Gospel of Repentance," Oct. 1982
Ezra Taft Benson, "Cleansing the Inner Vessel," May 1986
Boyd K. Packer, "I Will Remember Your Sins No More," May 2006
James E. Faust, "The Power to Change," Nov. 2007
Russell M. Nelson, "Jesus Christ—the Master Healer," Nov. 2005
David A. Bednar, "Clean Hands and a Pure Heart," Nov. 2007

NOTES:

WHO SHALL ASCEND INTO THE HILL OF THE LORD? WHO SHALL STAND IN HIS HOLY PLACE? HE THAT HATH CLEAN HANDS AND A PURE HEART. PSALM 24:3–4

WHO SHALL ASCEND INTO THE HILL OF THE LORD? WHO SHALL STAND IN HIS HOLY PLACE? HE THAT HATH CLEAN HANDS AND A PURE HEART. PSALM 24:3–4

WHO SHALL ASCEND INTO THE HILL OF THE LORD? WHO SHALL STAND IN HIS HOLY PLACE? HE THAT HATH CLEAN HANDS AND A PURE HEART. PSALM 24:3–4

WHO SHALL ASCEND INTO THE HILL OF THE LORD? WHO SHALL STAND IN HIS HOLY PLACE? HE THAT HATH CLEAN HANDS AND A PURE HEART. PSALM 24:3–4

LESSON TWENTY

BAPTISM

Hymns

"Lord, Accept into Thy Kingdom" — Hymns #236
"Come, Follow Me" — Hymns #116
"Father in Heaven, We Do Believe" — Hymns #180
"Jesus, Mighty King in Zion" — Hymns #234

SUMMARY:

To demonstrate our true repentance, we must follow the Savior and be baptized. Baptism by immersion for the remission of sins is an essential requirement for entry into the celestial kingdom. When we humble ourselves and are baptized, we receive the Holy Ghost and are admitted into the Lord's Church. Everyone is accountable for his actions at age eight and needs to enter into the baptismal covenant, which includes a promise to keep the commandments, serve God, stand as His witness, bear each other's burdens, and come into the fold of God.

QUOTES:

> "Baptism cleanses the soul from sin and prepares a person to lead a better, more perfect life in the future" (Theodore M. Burton, "To Be Born Again," *Ensign*, Sept. 1985, 66–70).

❧ "Faith and repentance, baptism and bestowal of the Holy Ghost constitute the heart of the gospel of Jesus Christ, being the essential requirements for entry into the celestial kingdom" (Bruce D. Porter, "The First Principles and Ordinances of the Gospel," *Ensign*, Oct. 2000, 8–15).

❧ "The full benefit of forgiveness of sin through the Savior's Atonement begins with repentance and baptism and then expands upon receiving the Holy Ghost" (James E. Faust, "Born Again," *Ensign*, May 2001, 54–55).

❧ "Baptism is the beginning of a new life for each one of us, a life of purpose," (Dwan J. Young, "Keeping the Covenants We Make at Baptism," *Ensign*, Nov. 1984, 94–95).

GOSPEL ART:

John the Baptist Baptizing Jesus – 208
Alma Baptizes in the Waters of Mormon – 309
Baptism – 601

OBJECT LESSONS:

❧ Ask the class if they would like some gum. When they express interest, pass out a plate with pieces of gum that have already been chewed, as well as pieces of gum still wrapped up "clean and pure." Act surprised when no one chooses the already chewed gum. Talk about how baptism washes us clean and makes us appear more presentable to the Lord.

❧ Show a hard boiled egg and explain that it represents how we all come to Earth: pure and unblemished. Draw all over the shell with crayons while you talk about the sins we make in life that tarnish us. (Don't use markers because they can bleed through the shell and ruin the visual effect!) Carefully peel the egg to show how baptism allows us to shed our worldly self and become pure and unblemished again.

ENSIGN TALKS:

Robert D. Hales, "The Covenant of Baptism: To Be In the Kingdom and Of the Kingdom," Nov. 2000

D. Todd Christofferson, "Born Again," May 2008

James E. Faust, "Born Again," May 2001

David E. Sorensen, "Why Baptism Is Not Enough," Apr. 1999

Theodore M. Burton, "To Be Born Again," Sept. 1985

Carol B. Thomas, "Spiritual Power of Our Baptism," May 1999

NOTES:

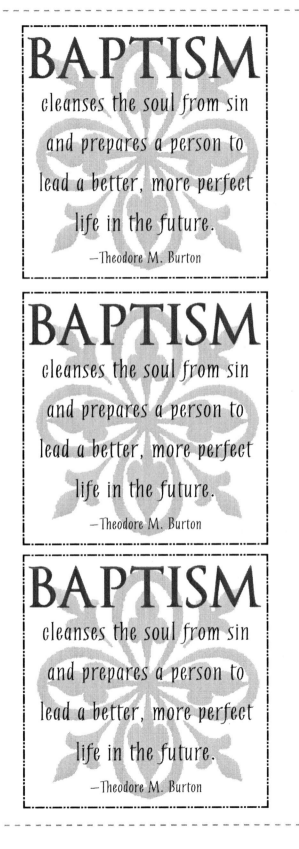

BAPTISM

cleanses the soul from sin
and prepares a person to
lead a better, more perfect
life in the future.

—Theodore M. Burton

BAPTISM

cleanses the soul from sin
and prepares a person to
lead a better, more perfect
life in the future.

—Theodore M. Burton

BAPTISM

cleanses the soul from sin
and prepares a person to
lead a better, more perfect
life in the future.

—Theodore M. Burton

LESSON TWENTY-ONE

THE GIFT OF THE HOLY GHOST

Hymns

"Behold Thy Sons and Daughters, Lord" — Hymns #238
"Dearest Children, God Is Near You" — Hymns #96
"God of Power, God of Right" — Hymns #20
"Great is the Lord" — Hymns #77
"Hear Thou Our Hymn, O Lord" — Hymns #222

SUMMARY:

The Holy Ghost is a member of the Godhead whose unique mission is to testify of Jesus Christ and God the Father. Everyone in the world can feel the influence of the Holy Ghost at certain times; however, the gift of the Holy Ghost is the privilege to receive its constant companionship and guidance. The gift of the Holy Ghost is bestowed upon a repentant person whose sins have been washed away at baptism. To hear the quiet promptings of the Holy Ghost we must be obedient, humble, and prayerful. This great gift from a loving Father can bless us with guidance, comfort, and testimony.

QUOTES:

- "If [we] would open [our] hearts to the refining influence of this unspeakable gift of the Holy Ghost, a glorious new spiritual dimension would come to light" (Joseph B. Wirthlin, "The Unspeakable Gift," *Ensign*, May 2003, 26–29).

- "This powerful gift entitles the leaders and all worthy members of the Church to enjoy the gifts and companionship of the Holy Ghost, a member of the Godhead whose function is to inspire, reveal, and teach all things" (James E. Faust, "Communion with the Holy Spirit," *Ensign*, Mar. 2002, 2–7).

- "We have been promised the constant companionship of the third member of the Godhead and hence the privilege of receiving revelation for our own lives" (Sheri L. Dew, "We Are Not Alone," *Ensign*, Nov. 1998, 94–96; or *Liahona*, Jan. 1999, 112–140).

GOSPEL ART:

Abinadi before King Noah – 308
Samuel the Lamanite on the Wall – 314
The Gift of the Holy Ghost – 602

OBJECT LESSONS:

- Demonstrate the difference between the influence of the Holy Ghost and the gift of the Holy Ghost by using a flashlight. Explain that everyone in the world can feel flashes of inspiration from the Holy Ghost at times when they are receiving comfort, guidance, or a witness of truth; however, it often quickly fades away. Make the flashlight go on and off. Then tell how after people are baptized and given the gift of the Holy Ghost, they have the privilege of having the Holy Ghost as a constant companion. Turn on the flashlight and keep it on. We can keep our spiritual "batteries" charged and receive continuous light from the Holy Ghost if we live worthily.

❧ Show a laptop computer and explain that it has a special device inside that allows it to pick up an Internet signal. If the computer is in range of the signal, it has the ability to receive information from all over the world. Explain how as baptized members of the Church, we have also been given a special device: the Holy Ghost. When we are in spiritual range, we can receive information from heaven! Talk about some of the things that help us stay in range, as well as those things which keep us from it. (See the handout that goes with this lesson for more ideas.)

❧ Before class, put water in a clear glass and put some hydrogen peroxide in another clear glass. They should look the same to your class members. Ask for a volunteer to dip an index finger on each hand into the two glasses. Now ask the volunteer to rub her fingers with each separate hand until the dipping fingers are dry. One should look the same, while the other one should have some white streaks on it (from the hydrogen peroxide). Ask the class "What is the chemical formula for water?" (H_2O). "What is the chemical formula for hydrogen peroxide?" (H_2O_2). How much difference does one oxygen molecule make? The water represents how we can all feel the Holy Ghost at certain times in our lives. The hydrogen peroxide shows how the gift of the Holy Ghost can stay with you.

ENSIGN TALKS:

Boyd K. Packer, "The Gift of the Holy Ghost: What Every Member Should Know," Aug. 2006

David A. Bednar, "That We May Always Have His Spirit to Be with Us," May 2006

James E. Faust, "The Gift of the Holy Ghost—A Sure Compass," Apr. 1996

James E. Faust, "Communion with the Holy Ghost," Mar. 2002

Dallin H. Oaks, "Spiritual Gifts," Sept. 1986

Neal A. Maxwell, "The Holy Ghost: Glorifying Christ," Jul. 2002

NOTES:

W E HAVE BEEN PROMISED THE CONSTANT **COMPANIONSHIP** OF THE THIRD MEMBER OF THE GODHEAD AND HENCE THE PRIVILEGE OF **RECEIVING** **REVELATION** FOR OUR OWN LIVES.

—SHERI L. DEW

W E HAVE BEEN PROMISED THE CONSTANT **COMPANIONSHIP** OF THE THIRD MEMBER OF THE GODHEAD AND HENCE THE PRIVILEGE OF **RECEIVING** **REVELATION** FOR OUR OWN LIVES.

—SHERI L. DEW

W E HAVE BEEN PROMISED THE CONSTANT **COMPANIONSHIP** OF THE THIRD MEMBER OF THE GODHEAD AND HENCE THE PRIVILEGE OF **RECEIVING** **REVELATION** FOR OUR OWN LIVES.

—SHERI L. DEW

W E HAVE BEEN PROMISED THE CONSTANT **COMPANIONSHIP** OF THE THIRD MEMBER OF THE GODHEAD AND HENCE THE PRIVILEGE OF **RECEIVING** **REVELATION** FOR OUR OWN LIVES.

—SHERI L. DEW

W E HAVE BEEN PROMISED THE CONSTANT **COMPANIONSHIP** OF THE THIRD MEMBER OF THE GODHEAD AND HENCE THE PRIVILEGE OF **RECEIVING** **REVELATION** FOR OUR OWN LIVES.

—SHERI L. DEW

W E HAVE BEEN PROMISED THE CONSTANT **COMPANIONSHIP** OF THE THIRD MEMBER OF THE GODHEAD AND HENCE THE PRIVILEGE OF **RECEIVING** **REVELATION** FOR OUR OWN LIVES.

—SHERI L. DEW

THE GIFTS OF THE SPIRIT

Hymns

"Be Thou Humble" — Hymns #130
"Come, Let Us Anew" — Hymns #217
"Scatter Sunshine" — Hymns #230
"You Can Make the Pathway Bright" — Hymns #228
"We Are Marching on to Glory" — Hymns #225

SUMMARY:

Father in Heaven sends each of us to Earth with certain spiritual gifts. When we are faithful and prayerful we can ask Him to bless us with additional gifts and powers in order to bless others and build His kingdom here on Earth. Some of the gifts we can study and ask for include the following: the gift of tongues; the ability to interpret tongues; the power of translation; wisdom; knowledge; effective teaching; testimony; the gift of believing the testimony of others; prophecy; healing; working of miracles; and powerful faith. To develop our gifts requires fasting, prayer, and humility. Satan can imitate certain gifts, so we need to be prayerful, discerning, and focused on Christ.

QUOTES:

- "It is up to each of us to search for and build upon the gifts which God has given" (Marvin J. Ashton, " 'There Are Many Gifts,' " *Ensign*, Nov. 1987, 20–23).

- "Spiritual gifts are blessings reserved to the faithful—not signs to the unbelieving" (Lane Johnson, "How to Receive Spiritual Gifts," *Ensign*, Dec. 1975, 46–47).

- "The gifts of the Spirit will come by the Holy Ghost. May [we] open [our] hearts to these gifts, seek them earnestly, live worthily to receive them, and use them for the benefit of all" (Relief Society General Presidency, "Seeking the Best Gifts," *Ensign*, Jan. 1997, 55).

- "Among the sure signs of the true church of Christ are the accompanying spiritual gifts" (James A. Cullimore, "Gifts of the Spirit," *Ensign*, Nov. 1974, 27–28).

GOSPEL ART:

Jesus Blesses the Nephite Children – 322

OBJECT LESSONS:

ᴂ Show the class a Swiss Army knife that has lots of different parts and ask them to identify their individual uses. They are all very useful, but each serves different functions. Their cause is the same: to make a more effective camper. So it is with spiritual gifts. None of them are more important than the others; rather, they all serve specific functions, and together, they all serve the purpose of building the kingdom of God!

ENSIGN TALKS:

Robert D. Hales, "Gifts of the Spirit," Feb. 2002
Henry B. Eyring, "Gifts of the Spirit for Hard Times," June 2007
Dallin H. Oaks, "Spiritual Gifts," Sept. 1986
Dieter F. Uchtdorf, "The Fruits of the First Vision," May 2005
James E. Faust, "Voice of the Spirit," June 2006
Lane Johnson, "How to Receive Spiritual Gifts," Dec. 1975
James A. Cullimore, "Gifts of the Spirit," Nov. 1974

NOTES:

THE GIFTS OF THE SPIRIT WILL COME BY THE HOLY
GHOST. MAY [WE] OPEN [OUR] HEARTS TO THESE GIFTS,
SEEK THEM EARNESTLY, LIVE WORTHILY TO RECEIVE
THEM, AND USE THEM FOR THE BENEFIT OF ALL.

—GENERAL RELIEF SOCIETY PRESIDENCY, 1997

My gifts & talents	How can I use them to bless others?

LESSON TWENTY-THREE

THE SACRAMENT

Hymns

"In Memory of the Crucified" — Hymns #190
"While of These Emblems We Partake" — Hymns #173, #174
"He Died! The Great Redeemer Died" — Hymns #192
"God Loved Us, So He Sent His Son" — Hymns #187
"Again We Meet Around the Board" — Hymns #186
"Father in Heaven, We Do Believe" — Hymns #180
"We'll Sing All Hail to Jesus' Name" — Hymns #182

SUMMARY:

The sacrament is an ordinance designed by the Lord to help us remember His atoning sacrifice and the hope we have in Him of returning to live with our Father in Heaven. It is full of rich symbolism and offers an opportunity to renew our baptismal covenants, which also incorporate the same symbols. The bread represents the Savior's body, which was ransomed for us on the cross and later resurrected in glory. The wine (water) causes our mind to reflect on the blood that was shed for our sins and by which we are atoned for our sins. By partaking of the sacrament each week at church, we are remembering our covenants and that through Christ, we too can overcome physical and spiritual death.

QUOTES:

᷉ "When we partake of the sacrament with a sincere heart, with real intent, forsaking our sins, and renewing our commitment to God, the Lord provides a way whereby sins can be forgiven" (Vaughn J. Featherstone, "Sacrament Meeting and the Sacrament," *Ensign*, Sept. 2001, 23–25).

᷉ "As we worthily partake of the sacrament, we will sense those things we need to improve in and receive the help and determination to do so. No matter what our problems, the sacrament always gives hope" (John H. Groberg, "The Beauty and Importance of the Sacrament," *Ensign*, May 1989, 38–40).

᷉ "Reminding us weekly of our need to foster charity toward our fellow Saints, the sacrament can be a great force for unity in our congregations" (John S. Tanner, "Reflections on the Sacrament Prayers," *Ensign*, Apr. 1986, 7–11)

᷉ As we partake of the sacrament, "our witness that we are willing to take upon us the name of Jesus Christ constitutes our declaration of candidacy for exaltation in the celestial kingdom" (Dallin H. Oaks, "Taking upon Us the Name of Jesus Christ," *Ensign*, May 1985, 80–83).

GOSPEL ART:

Jesus Washing the Apostles' Feet – 226
Jesus Praying in Gethsemane – 227
The Crucifixion – 230
Jesus' Tomb – 232
Mary and the Resurrected Lord – 233

OBJECT LESSONS:

❧ Prepare a pane of clear glass or picture frame that is dirty on one side and show it to the class. Explain to the class that sometimes we don't even realize how dirty we're getting from the world (inside and out) because it accumulates over time. Use a glass cleaner wipe to clear away some of the dirt on the glass. Explain that by coming to church and partaking of the sacrament, we can become unspotted from the world and have clearer vision. Read D&C 59:9 and discuss with the class.

ENSIGN TALKS:

L. Tom Perry, "As Now We Take the Sacrament," May 2006
Dallin H. Oaks, "Sacrament Meeting and the Sacrament," Nov. 2008
Russell M. Nelson, "Worshiping at Sacrament Meeting," Aug. 2004
David B. Haight, "The Sacrament—and the Sacrifice," Apr. 2007
David B. Haight, "Remembering the Savior's Atonement," Apr. 1988
W. Mack Lawrence, "Sunday Worship Service," May 1991

NOTES:

SACRAMENT

"AS WE WORTHILY PARTAKE OF THE SACRAMENT, WE WILL SENSE THOSE THINGS WE NEED TO IMPROVE IN AND RECEIVE THE HELP AND THE DETERMINATION TO DO SO. NO MATTER WHAT OUR PROBLEMS, THE SACRAMENT ALWAYS GIVES HOPE."
—JOHN H. GROBERG

SACRAMENT

"AS WE WORTHILY PARTAKE OF THE SACRAMENT, WE WILL SENSE THOSE THINGS WE NEED TO IMPROVE IN AND RECEIVE THE HELP AND THE DETERMINATION TO DO SO. NO MATTER WHAT OUR PROBLEMS, THE SACRAMENT ALWAYS GIVES HOPE."
—JOHN H. GROBERG

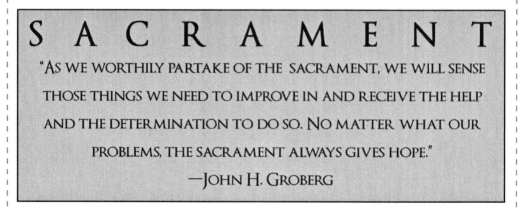

SACRAMENT

"AS WE WORTHILY PARTAKE OF THE SACRAMENT, WE WILL SENSE THOSE THINGS WE NEED TO IMPROVE IN AND RECEIVE THE HELP AND THE DETERMINATION TO DO SO. NO MATTER WHAT OUR PROBLEMS, THE SACRAMENT ALWAYS GIVES HOPE."
—JOHN H. GROBERG

THE SABBATH DAY

Hymns

"Sabbath Day" — Hymns #148
"Gently Raise The Sacred Strain" — Hymns #146
"Sabbath Day" — Hymns #148
"We Meet, Dear Lord" — Hymns #151
"O Thou Kind and Gracious Father" — Hymns #150
"Welcome, Welcome, Sabbath Morning" — Hymns #280

SUMMARY:

God ordained the Sabbath to be kept holy and declared it to be a day of rest from our labors. The Sabbath occurs every seven days and is designed to direct our thoughts away from the world and to focus on the Lord instead. In the beginning, God consecrated the seventh day to represent God's day of rest after He created the world. After Christ's resurrection, the first day of the week was honored as the Sabbath to commemorate His resurrection and symbolize how it is the Savior who truly gives us rest. A helpful guideline in determining whether an activity is appropriate for the Sabbath is to ask the following questions: Will it draw me closer to God? Does it show respect and love for the Savior? Will it inspire me and direct my thoughts to the Lord?

QUOTES:

ᴥ "Now is the time to ask ourselves: Is the Sabbath a holy day or a holiday? Shall I worship the Lord or worship pleasures and recreation?" (Charles Didier, "The Sabbath—Holy Day or Holiday?" *Ensign*, Oct. 1994, 26–31).

ᴥ "Our observance of the Sabbath is an indication of the depth of our conversion and our willingness to keep sacred covenants" (Earl C. Tingey, "The Sabbath Day and Sunday Shopping" *Ensign*, May 1996, 10–12).

ᴥ "There is a sure protection for ourselves and our children against the plague of our day. The key to that sure protection surprisingly can be found in Sabbath observance" (James E. Faust, "The Lord's Day," *Ensign*, Nov. 1991, 33–35).

OBJECT LESSONS:

ᴥ Invite someone in the class to enjoy an ice cream sundae with you. Dish out some ice cream and comment on how excited everyone looks about the yummy treat. Now put on various toppings such as pepperoni, BBQ sauce, chopped onions, and grated cheese. The class will probably express disgust. Ask them why they don't want those toppings. They'll probably say that they like those ingredients but not on top of a sundae. Talk about how choosing activities appropriate for Sunday is the same: activities we do during the week aren't bad activities, just not appropriate for the Sabbath day.

ᴥ Ask for a volunteer to put some white sugar into a clear glass, representing the Sabbath Day (clean and white). Now ask her to add some hot chocolate mix on top, representing the rest of the week. The class will see a definite line, dividing the two colors. Now ask the student to mix them up together. Explain how the Lord asks us to set apart the Sabbath Day to make it different than the rest of the week.

ENSIGN TALKS:

Ezra Taft Benson, "Keeping the Sabbath Day Holy," May 1971

H. Aldridge Gillespie, "The Blessing of Keeping the Sabbath Day Holy," Nov. 2000

John H. Groberg, "The Power of Keeping the Sabbath Day Holy," Nov. 1984

James E. Faust, "The Lord's Day," Nov. 1991

Earl C. Tingey, "Keeping the Sabbath Day Holy," Feb. 2000

Charles Didier, "The Sabbath—Holy Day or Holiday?" Oct. 1994

NOTES:

Helpful questions to ask when trying to decide if an activity is appropriate for the Sabbath Day:

Will it guide me closer to God?

Does it show respect and love for the Savior?

Will it inspire me?

Will it direct my thoughts to the Lord?

Will it help me keep the commandments?

" A world without a Sabbath would be like a man without a smile, like a summer without flowers, and like a homestead without a garden. It is the joyous day of the whole week."
—Henry Ward Beecher

Helpful questions to ask when trying to decide if an activity is appropriate for the Sabbath Day:

Will it guide me closer to God?

Does it show respect and love for the Savior?

Will it inspire me?

Will it direct my thoughts to the Lord?

Will it help me keep the commandments?

" A world without a Sabbath would be like a man without a smile, like a summer without flowers, and like a homestead without a garden. It is the joyous day of the whole week."
—Henry Ward Beecher

Helpful questions to ask when trying to decide if an activity is appropriate for the Sabbath Day:

Will it guide me closer to God?

Does it show respect and love for the Savior?

Will it inspire me?

Will it direct my thoughts to the Lord?

Will it help me keep the commandments?

" A world without a Sabbath would be like a man without a smile, like a summer without flowers, and like a homestead without a garden. It is the joyous day of the whole week."
—Henry Ward Beecher

Helpful questions to ask when trying to decide if an activity is appropriate for the Sabbath Day:

Will it guide me closer to God?

Does it show respect and love for the Savior?

Will it inspire me?

Will it direct my thoughts to the Lord?

Will it help me keep the commandments?

" A world without a Sabbath would be like a man without a smile, like a summer without flowers, and like a homestead without a garden. It is the joyous day of the whole week."
—Henry Ward Beecher

ABOUT THE AUTHOR

Trina Boice grew up in California. In 2004 she was honored as the California Young Mother of the Year, an award that completely amuses her four sons. She earned two bachelor's degrees from BYU, where she competed on the speech and debate team and the ballroom dance team, winning national titles for both. She was president of the National Honor Society Phi Eta Sigma and served as ASBYU secretary of student community services.

Trina also studied at the University of Salamanca in Spain and later returned there to serve an LDS mission in Madrid for one and a half years. She has a real estate license, travel agent license, two master's degrees, and a black belt in Tae Kwon Do, although she's the first to admit she'd pass out from fright if she were ever really attacked by a bad guy.

She worked as a legislative assistant for a congressman in Washington D.C., and was given the Points of Light Award and Presidential Volunteer Service Award for her domestic and international community service. She wrote a column called "The Boice Box" for a newspaper in Georgia, where she lived for fifteen years. She taught Spanish at a private high school and ran an appraisal business with her husband for twenty years. She currently writes for Roots Television and Go2.com and is the executive marketing director for Multi-Pure International.

Trina was selected by KPBS in San Diego to be a political correspondent during the last election year. If she told you what she really did, she'd have to kill you.

A popular and entertaining speaker, Trina is the author of seven books and can't wait to write her next one! You can read more about her books and upcoming events at www.boicebox.com.